Seven Steps to Homework Success
A Family Guide for
Solving Common Homework Problems

Sydney S. Zentall, Ph.D.
Sam Goldstein, Ph.D.

Illustrated by
Richard A. DiMatteo

Specialty Press, Inc.
Plantation, Florida

ISBN 1-886941-22-X

Library of Congress Cataloging-in-Publication Data

Zentall, Sydney S., 1943—

  Seven steps to homework success : a family guide for solving
common homework problems / Sydney S. Zentall, Sam Goldstein :
illustrated by Richard A. DiMatteo.
    p. cm.

  Includes bibliographical references (p.) and index.
  ISBN 1-886941-22-X
  1. Homework Handbooks, manuals, etc. 2. Study skills Handbooks,
manuals, ets. 3. Education--Parent participation Handbooks,
manuals, etc.   I. Goldstein, Sam, 1952—   . II. Title.
LB1048.Z45   1999
371.3'028'1--dc21   99-28621
                CIP

Cover Design by Todd Pernsteiner and Encompass Marketing
Copyedited by Dara Kates

10 9 8 7 6 5 4 3 2 1

Printed in the United States of America

Specialty Press, Inc.
300 Northwest 70th Avenue, Suite 102
Plantation, Florida 33317
(954) 792-8100 • (800) 233-9273
www.addwarehouse.com

Dedication

*To the significant teachers in my life—
my children, Gabe and Shannon. With
additional gratitude to Arlene Hall, who kindled
my interest in this important area through her doctoral
dissertation and our joint development of the Learning Station™.
…Sydney S. Zentall, Ph.D.*

*For my children, Allyson and Ryan.
Their dedication to education has been a joy to behold.
…Sam Goldstein, Ph.D.*

TABLE OF CONTENTS

INTRODUCTION
Seven Steps to Homework Success

Introduction
Seven Steps to Homework Success

A Visit to Elm Street

If you are like most parents, you may feel a mixture of emotions about your child's homework—some of them positive and some negative. Most of us didn't like doing homework when we were kids, and we probably don't like it any better as parents.

Nevertheless, homework, you are reminded by your children's teachers, is an important component of the school experience. You are told that completing homework successfully makes for successful students. Homework has and continues to be an institution in our educational system. But how much do we really know about homework, its purpose, its importance, and its value? How much do we know about parents' and children's experiences with homework or teachers' and administrators' goals? How many families find homework a successful, easy, mu-

tually reinforcing experience? How many dread homework? Consider a walk down Elm Street.

The Jones Family. It is 7:30 p.m. one Monday night in November. Most of the homes on Elm Street are brightly lit, dinner is over, and many children begin their homework. In the Jones' home, Mrs. Jones prepares to sit down with her eight-year-old son Robert. They enjoy completing homework together. Robert works diligently, showing his mother each math problem as it is completed.

The Smith Family. At the Smith household next door, 12-year-old Erica and her father dread homework. Since elementary school, homework has been a source of conflict for Erica and her family. Although Erica's academic achievement is quite good, she has never been interested in homework. She describes homework as boring. Over the years, Erica's parents have utilized a variety of rewards and punishments in an effort to motivate her. Her parents and teachers know Erica can complete homework on her own, however, they cannot motivate her to work independently. Even now, as Erica and her father sit down to complete homework, Erica starts her usual complaints. This time she is trying to convince her father that the homework isn't due tomorrow and could wait a few more days. Erica's parents worry that her lack of initiative will negatively impact her achievement.

The Sweeney Family. Down the street in the Sweeney household, Josh and his older sister sit down to complete spelling homework. Josh has struggled to learn to spell and is receiving special services at school. Although he tries very hard, he appears to forget words that he seemed to know just a few minutes before. Josh's sister has volunteered to help him with his spelling homework because his parents find working with him particularly stressful.

The Cunningham Family. The Cunninghams have three children. Each one's style of doing homework is as different as night and day. Eight-year-old Emily likes to complete homework in the kitchen but is easily distracted by her envi-

ronment (e.g., phone ringing, people talking). Her parents suspect this is why she wants to complete homework in the kitchen in the first place. Eleven-year-old Andrew prefers completing homework in front of the television. His homework often contains many mistakes and his parents are concerned that the television is distracting. It appears that 14-year-old Susan completes homework between taking phone calls from multiple friends, listening to her stereo, and trying on clothes. Mr. and Mrs. Cunningham aren't sure what to do about their children's different homework habits.

The Roberts Family. Across the street, 15-year-old Angela begins to do her homework. Angela is in her room, the door is closed, and the radio is blaring. Mr. and Mrs. Roberts question if she is actually doing her work, but they must wait until her grades appear to learn whether Angela's reports of completed homework are accurate. They wonder how they can establish better communication with Angela's teachers so they can monitor homework more closely. They disagree with one another, however, as to how involved they should be.

As these examples illustrate, children differ a great deal in their attitudes about homework and the methods they use to get it done. Even in well-functioning families, under ideal circumstances, homework can be one of the hottest parent-child crisis buttons. Parents are unsure as to the best time, place, routine, or system their kids should use to do homework. Many children rebel, and parents feel overwhelmed by the pressure of meeting their children's school demands. It is not surprising that parents complain about homework almost as much as their children do. Many cite it as the number one problem in their household. In extreme cases, families report that for 10 months a year their lives revolve around homework.

For children experiencing school problems, the challenges of homework are added to existing classroom difficulties. It is not uncommon for these children to bring incomplete classwork home as homework. For them, there is the prospect of hours and hours of school work at home, often with minimal long-term benefit.

Most children during their school career forget some assignments, lose homework, require assistance with homework, and make mistakes on homework. Some children have difficulty learning essential skills, which enable them to complete homework independently. They may have trouble getting assignments. They may not have an appropriate place at home to complete homework. They may become confused over starting their homework because of problems following directions. Some children are overwhelmed by long-term projects or difficult homework assignments. They don't know how to break the assignments down into smaller steps for completion. Children who rush through assignments without checking their work may earn poor grades on homework. Some children have trouble returning completed homework to school on time.

Our goal in writing this workbook is to show parents how they can teach their child important homework skills. We will also suggest positive practices that parents and teachers can use to promote homework success. Based on our combined years of research and experience with thousands of families, we have developed a practical, hands-on, seven step program to reduce homework problems. As far as we are aware, this is the first volume to combine proven research with practical suggestions.

The chapters in this workbook represent the seven sequential steps necessary to achieve homework success in your family. Take a moment and review the seven steps.

Seven Steps
to Homework Success

1. Understand the Importance of Homework in Your Child's Education

In the first step we explain the purposes of homework and its role in your child's education. We are convinced that the value your child places on homework will come, in part, from the value you place on homework. With the understanding that homework is important, you will be in a better position to motivate yourself and your child.

2. Your Child's Homework Skills

In this step we identify seven important skills your child needs to be able to manage homework. This chapter starts with the "Inventory of Homework Skills" to help you and your child evaluate your child's areas of strength and weakness. Then specific recommendations are provided to strengthen weak skills.

3. Developing a Homework Alliance with Your Child

Ideally, you would like your children to complete homework accurately, completely, on time, and on their own. Believe it or not, some kids can achieve this goal consistently. It is likely that their parents are not reading this workbook. They are probably relaxing or having fun. Other kids, for whatever reason, need help with their homework. And parents are usually the best source of help available. We firmly believe that the type of relationship or alliance parents develop with their child with regard to homework can be very beneficial. In this step we ask you to self-analyze. This will help you better understand yourself and how your family operates. We focus on the things you can do to help your child be more successful in school.

4. Common Homework Problems and How to Solve Them

The stress of completing homework can cause a great deal of family tension. Many parents and children find themselves repeating specific patterns of behavior centering around homework. These are nonproductive and damaging to family relationships. In this step we identify eleven common homework problems and provide solutions. It is important for you to identify whether these problems exist in your family as you develop a homework plan.

5. Building the Learning Station™

In step five we will teach you how to build and begin using the Learning Station™, a free standing, three-sided panel. Children using the Learning Station™ increase the amount of homework completed independently and do so with greater accuracy.

6. Effective Home-School Communication

Consistent, effective communication between you and your child's teachers is critical to helping your child manage homework. Whether it be by phone, note, or e-mail, good communication is essential. In step six we will provide you with tips and guidelines to open and maintain lines of communication with school personnel.

7. What Parent's Should Know About Homework Assignments

Teachers struggle with homework, too. Although homework has been identified as an essential component of teaching, there are no university courses in homework. Teachers are often left to their own ideas and devices in determining type, quantity, and schedule of homework. We will provide you with empirically-based instructional methods that teachers have found to improve student homework production. You can offer these helpful suggestions about homework to your child's teachers. Remove the perforated Special Addendum entitled "A Brief Teacher's Guide to Homework" and give it to your child's teachers.

When you turn the next page, you will take the first step to helping your child become more independent, savvy, and successful in completing homework. As you work through each step in this workbook, you will move closer to homework success in your home. We have included a checklist to help you track each step as it is accomplished. Good luck.

Seven Steps to Homework Success in Your Home

Use this checklist to track your progress as you go through the seven steps in this workbook.

✔1. I understand that homework is important, and I am committed to helping my child be successful.

✔2. I know the seven skills my child needs to use to be successful with homework, and I know how to help my child improve these skills.

✔3. I recognize the positive things I can do as a parent to improve my child's school work.

✔4. I understand and recognize common homework problems that can arise in families, and I know how to solve them.

✔5. We have built the Learning Station™, and it is ready to go.

✔6. I have established effective communication with my child's teachers.

✔7. I understand and have available a variety of tips to offer my child's teachers when homework problems arise.

Summary

If you are experiencing homework problems in your home, you are not alone. It is our hope that as you read this book you will find solutions to these problems. The strategies and ideas you will read about are based on empirical research and practical experience. We are confident that following these seven steps will lead to homework success in your home. Our goal is to help your child take responsibility for homework and learn the skills necessary to complete homework independently.

STEP 1
Understanding the Importance
of Homework in Your Child's Education

Step 1
Understanding the Importance of Homework in Your Child's Education

In response to homework difficulties, some parents quickly dismiss the importance of homework. They conclude that it is busy work unsuited to the learning needs of their children and not worth the stress and irritation it causes. As one parent noted, "homework has dominated and ruined our lives for the past eight years."[1] Yet before we dismiss the importance of homework, let's examine what homework is, why it is important, and some of the most common problems reported.

What is Homework?

Everyone can define homework. The definition is simple: Homework is the additional activities assigned to students, which are meant to be carried out during non-school hours.[2] Homework, whether it is reading, writing, recording observations of nature, or something as simple as watching a program, is a task assigned to students by teachers. It is meant to further the education of students. However, the very word causes dissatisfaction in the minds of students, anticipation of conflict in the minds of parents, and the promise of additional management and supervision for wayward students in the minds of teachers.

As far as we are aware, no one has written the definitive history of homework. We do not know by whom or when the first homework assignment was given. We would not be surprised, however, to learn that whether this occurred 100, 1,000 or 5,000 years ago that the very first homework assignment was received similarly to homework assignments given to your children today.

Why is Homework Important?

Homework is important because it is at the intersection between home and school. It serves as a window through which you can observe your children's education and express positive attitudes toward your children and their education. As children get older, homework and the amount of time engaged in homework increases in importance. For teachers and administrators, homework is a cost-effective way to provide additional instruction and practice.

Let's examine the purposes of homework. We summarize six constructive purposes for homework in the context of your child's educational experiences.[3] The first two are the most important and obvious. Through (1) *practice* and (2) *participation in learning tasks*, homework will improve your child's achievement. Thus, it would be expected that if homework were completed accurately, not only would your child's general knowledge and grades improve, but your child would also increase mastery of basic academic skills (e.g., reading, writing, spelling, and mathematics).

Homework can provide other benefits. Your child's ability to bring an assignment home, gather and organize the necessary materials to complete the assignment, return the assignment, and receive a grade, strengthens your child's sense of responsibility. Time management skills

are learned. There is improved (3) *development of personal skills*, such as responsibility and time management, gained by completing homework. Further, when homework proceeds smoothly, it can become a (4) *positive aspect of your relationship with your child*.

Finally, although we often do not consider that homework serves a school administrative role, it offers schools an opportunity to let parents know what their children are learning. Thus, homework can play a public relations role by (5) *keeping parents informed* about class activities and policies. Homework can also fulfill (6) *an administrative role* in helping the school achieve its overall mission of improving students' achievement.

Homework is a bridge that joins schools and parents. From the school's perspective, there is the opportunity to monitor students' independent progress. For parents, there is the potential to gain a greater appreciation of education and to express positive attitudes toward their children and achievement.

Does Time Engaged in Homework Produce Gains?

Recent research studies find that some home-work practices (e.g., use of feedback) improves students' grades.[4] However, the gains are less consistent when looking at year-end achievement. At younger grade levels, there is little relation between the amount of time devoted to homework and achievement.[4] On the other hand, in the upper grades, the more time spent on homework, the greater achievement gains. By the high school years, nearly two-thirds of teachers provide homework assignments two to four times per week.

Although homework is important at all ages, at younger ages, in particular, you need to help your child establish a balance between time spent on homework and other home activities. This is particularly true if your child is receiving special services or is learning disabled. In this case, it is likely your child is delayed in achievement, and teachers may attempt to help them "catch up" by providing extra homework. Because it is important to emphasize school and homework during these years, it is tempting to view non-school activities (e.g., playing, interacting with friends, or participating in organized activities such as boy scouts) as insignificant. We know, however,

they are of equal importance and time must be allotted to them.

How Much Time Should Be Spent on Homework?

Researchers suggest that the amount of time students should be expected to work on homework are as follows:[5]

Elementary students. At the elementary level, we suggest that homework is brief, at your child's ability level, and involves frequent, voluntary, and high interest activities. These students need high levels of feedback and/or supervision so they can do their assignments correctly. This is why in-class study periods can be more valuable than homework at this age level.[6] During in-class study, your child may receive more feedback from adults or peers than is available at home.

Completing homework correctly is influenced by your child's ability, the difficulty of the task, and the amount of feedback one receives. When assigning homework, your child's teachers may struggle to create a balance between ability, task difficulty, and feedback. Unfortunately, there are no simple guiding principles. We can assure you, however, that your input and feedback on a

Time Spent On Homework

Grade	# Assignments	TimeRequired
1 to 3	1 - 3 per week	15 minutes
4 to 6	2 - 4 per week	15-45 minutes
7 to 9	3 - 5 sets per week	45-75 minutes per set
10 to 12	4 - 5 sets per week	75-150 minutes per set

nightly basis is an *essential* component in helping your child benefit from the homework experience. In fact, one research study found that fourth through sixth graders receiving parental feedback on a regular basis while completing homework obtained better test scores than students in similar classes without such homework and feedback.[7]

Junior high and high school students. For students in middle and high school grades, there are greater overall benefits from time engaged in practicing and thinking about school work. These benefits do not appear to depend as much upon immediate supervision or feedback as they do for elementary students. The average high school student, when assigned homework in a class, outperformed two thirds of peers in a non-homework class as measured by standardized tests.[8] Junior high students achieved half that gain. The gains that have been reported from homework at the older age levels may be due to the fact time spent doing homework represents a significant amount (about 20 percent) of the overall time students are engaged with their academic tasks.

Thus, as children get older, homework and the amount of time engaged in homework increases in importance. Due to the significance of homework at the older age levels, it is not surprising that there is more homework assigned. Furthermore, homework is almost always assigned in college preparatory classes and assigned at least three quarters of the time in special education and vocational training classes. Thus, at any age, homework may indicate our academic expectations of children.

Regardless of the amount of homework assigned, many students unsuccessful or struggling in school, spend less rather than more time engaged in homework.[9] It is not surprising that

students who spend less time completing homework may eventually not achieve as consistently as those who complete their homework.[10] Does this mean that time devoted to homework is the key component necessary for achievement? We are not completely certain. Some American educators have concluded that if students in America spent as much time doing homework as students in Asian countries, they might perform academically as well. It is tempting to assume such a cause and effect relationship. However, this relationship appears to be an overly simple conclusion. We know that homework is important as one of several influential factors in school success.

Other variables, including student ability, achievement, motivation, and teaching quality, influence the time students will spend with homework tasks. Many students and their parents have told us that they experience less difficulty being motivated and completing homework in classes in which they enjoy the subject, the instruction, the assignments, and the teachers.

The benefits from homework are the greatest for students who complete the most homework and who do so correctly.[11] Thus, students who devote time to homework are probably on a path to improved achievement. This path also includes higher quality instruction, greater achievement motivation, and better skill levels.

What Types of Assignments are Students Given?

The most frequently assigned types of homework for elementary, middle, and high schools are:

- ✎ unfinished classwork (51 percent);
- ✎ practice (22 percent);
- ✎ enrichment or make-up when a child

missed school (9 percent); and
✎ preparation for upcoming classwork (6 percent) or for a test (4 percent).[12]

Teachers across all grade levels rate preparation for tests and practice of skills already taught as the most helpful types of assignments.[13] Enrichment activities and preparation for future classwork are rated as less helpful.

Unfortunately, the types of homework that teachers think are helpful may not be consistent with today's changing view of learning. Increasingly, the focus today is on students developing understanding through experience and discovery (e.g., to develop their own position on the question of why dinosaurs became extinct).[14] These different types of assignments will require your role to change somewhat from helping your children complete worksheets, read, or memorize material to guiding them in the application of knowledge and in discovery thinking. You are probably most familiar with practice assignments and those that help your child prepare for new lessons. You may have less experience with creative assignments or those requiring transfer of learning to new settings. For example, a teacher assigned children the task of identifying many different ways to solve several math problems. Unfortunately, she found that her students were reinstructed by their parents to do all of the problems "the right way."[15] Even though parents may be less familiar with these types of divergent thinking homework tasks, such creative and experiential assignments are often hands-on and can be quite enjoyable for you and your child.

In high school settings, where assignments could be more varied and address the higher order skills of application and creativity (e.g., es-says, book reports, diaries, research reports, projects), the range of homework is actually narrower. Teachers usually assign two types of homework: (1) textbooks with questions and (2) worksheets.[16] Boredom can play a greater role at older age levels. For example, more 7th through 9th graders reported boredom during homework than 5th and 6th graders.[17, 18] Boredom could also explain the findings that (a) approximately half of all high school students complete less than 80 percent of their work and (b) only about 40 percent of students achieve expected accuracy rates of 80 to 100 percent correct, even though most assignments were practice types of tasks.[19]

The need for greater variety of assignments was expressed by one parent who commented, "In social studies and science he gets 'fun' projects, but the math teacher works right out of the book. It has really turned my son off."[20] The importance of tasks that hold students' interest has been well demonstrated. For example, fast paced computer programs with multiple choice questions, in comparison to traditional homework tasks, have been found to raise the potential of students over what was predicted by their standardized test scores.[21]

Complaints Teachers, Parents, and Students Have about Homework

Since researchers cannot enter hundreds of homes to understand the problems and processes that contribute to homework failure, most researchers interview teachers, parents, and students to determine common homework problems.

Complaints About Homework

Common Teacher Complaints
- Student's fail to complete assigned homework.
- Students are not interested/do not care about homework.
- Homework may lead to reduced motivation in class.
- Valuable classroom time may be consumed in collecting and correcting homework.
- There is a lack of commitment by parents to the homework process.

Common Parent Complaints
- They are inconsistently informed of homework assignments.
- They may not always understand the purposes of homework.
- They are confused about the specific role teachers expect them to play.

Common Student Complaints
- Homework is unfinished because it is either too difficult or too boring.
- Homework assignments are too long.
- Homework is often just a repetition of what they did in class.
- Homework denies them access to play and community activities.

In the early grades, short, successful, high interest, homework assignments that can be completed with family members are the most beneficial. In the late elementary years, your involvement by providing supervision and feedback helps your children achieve and may set the foundation for successful completion of homework in high school. The amount of time spent on homework increases as your child progresses into high school. Here the benefits of homework are greatest for students who complete the most homework and do so correctly.

As our goals for education and our view of learning advances, you must not only help your child complete homework in the form of worksheets, reading, or memorization of material, but also act as a facilitator. This means helping your child think creatively and complete homework assignments that teach problem solving and divergent thinking.

Homework is important in your child's education, and it is here to stay. In fact, from 1930 to 1950, students studied no more than 60 to 120 minutes per week outside of school. Students in 1986 in grades 6 to 12 were spending an average of 80 minutes per night on homework.[22]   You are now ready to proceed to step two—Your Child's Homework Skills.

Summary

We hope the information in this chapter has helped you better understand homework, the important role homework plays in your child's education, and how homework can benefit your child.

STEP 2
Your Child's Homework Skills

Step 2
Your Child's Homework Skills

The goal of this workbook is to help your child develop the skills and responsibility necessary to complete homework independently. To begin, it is important to obtain a clear understanding of your child's homework skills. We have identified seven essential skills which we think are necessary for children to learn and practice to manage their homework.

Seven Essential Homework Skills

✎1. Record the assignment given by the teacher and bring home the proper books and supplies.

✎2. Choose an appropriate place in which to complete homework.

✎3. Start assignments by reading directions and follow them carefully.

✎4. Manage difficult or long-term assignments.

✎5. Maintain attention when assignments are boring.

✎6. Check work to make certain it is accurate and thorough.

✎7. Return homework to school and turn it in when it is due.

Take an Inventory of Your Child's Homework Skills

On the next two pages is the "Inventory of Homework Skills." Your child may complete this independently or you and your child may complete it together. This inventory focuses on the seven homework skills listed above. Young children will need your help in reading this inventory and answering the questions. You may have to read it to them and rephrase certain questions to help them understand. Older children should have no difficulty completing the inventory on their own. However, keep in mind that a child's self-report may not be an accurate indication of how they really behave in different circumstances. If your child is able to complete this inventory alone, you may want to complete the "Positive Parenting Homework Practices" questionnaire in step 3 at the same time.

THE INVENTORY OF HOMEWORK SKILLS

Name of Child _____   Date _____

Answer each question by marking a check in either the "Yes" or "No" column. Score one point for each "Yes" answer.

1.   Writes down the correct assignment given by the teacher and brings home the proper books and supplies.

_____ Yes _____ No   1.   Do you know <u>when</u> your teacher(s) typically give homework (e.g., every day, certain days, before class begins, at the end of class)?

_____ Yes _____ No   2.   Do you know <u>how</u> your teacher(s) typically give homework (e.g., verbally, on the board, written on pieces of paper)?

_____ Yes _____ No   3.   Do you write your assignments in an assignment book or a homework planner?

_____ Yes _____ No   4.   Do you get the materials (books, assignments) you need from school to home?

_____ Yes _____ No   5.   Do you keep track of all your assignments and their due dates?

Category Score_____

2.   Chooses an appropriate place in which to do homework.

_____ Yes _____ No   1.   Do you have a favorite "homework place" where you can concentrate?

_____ Yes _____ No   2.   Do you have the proper school work materials (paper, pencils, rulers, etc.) available in your "homework place?"

_____ Yes _____ No   3.   Do you have a way of keeping your school work/materials organized?

_____ Yes _____ No   4.   Do you usually start your homework at a specific time each day?

_____ Yes _____ No   5.   Do you change things around in your homework place from time to time to see if you study better under different conditions (e.g., with and without music playing, lighting changes, at a desk)?

Category Score_____

3.   Starts assignments by reading directions and following them carefully.

_____ Yes _____ No   1.   Do you usually read directions before starting an assignment?

_____ Yes _____ No   2.   Do you ask for help when you do not understand what to do?

_____ Yes _____ No   3.   Do you have the phone number of another student (or a teacher) in each class to call if you need help with an assignment?

_____ Yes _____ No   4.   If you are stuck on an assignment and cannot get help, do you try to figure it out on your own or ask a teacher for help the next day?

_____ Yes _____ No   5.   Do you look for examples in the book or from class notes to help you understand how to do an assignment?

Category Score_____

4. Manages difficult or long-term assignments.

____ Yes ____ No   1. Do you write down long-term assignments and the steps to complete these assignments on a calendar or a list?

____ Yes ____ No   2. Before beginning a difficult assignment, do you underline or use markers to highlight key words in the directions, computational signs and key words in math, or main ideas in reading and social studies?

____ Yes ____ No   3. Do you take breaks so you don't get too tired on difficult or long assignments?

____ Yes ____ No   4. Do you have ways to remember important information such as writing down key ideas, drawing pictures, making diagrams?

____ Yes ____ No   5. Do you make up questions for yourself or write brief summaries while preparing for a test?

Category Score_____

5. Maintains attention when assignments are boring

____ Yes ____ No   1. Do you spend enough time on homework even if it is boring?

____ Yes ____ No   2. Do you usually finish your homework even if it is boring?

____ Yes ____ No   3. Do you take breaks from boring assignments and come back to them at a later time?

____ Yes ____ No   4. Do you reward yourself when you reach certain goals.

____ Yes ____ No   5. Do you try to make a boring assignment "fun" (e.g., make a game out of it)?

Category Score_____

6. Checks work for thoroughness and accuracy.

____ Yes ____ No   1. Do you check your assignment book to make sure you have completed all the homework assigned for that day?

____ Yes ____ No   2. Do you put the appropriate headings on your papers?

____ Yes ____ No   3. Do you write neatly?

____ Yes ____ No   4. Do you check each problem or question to make sure you have answered it correctly?

____ Yes ____ No   5. Do you ask someone else to check your work to make sure you have done the assignment correctly?

Category Score_____

7. Returns homework to school when it is due.

____ Yes ____ No   1. Do you take your completed homework back to school?

____ Yes ____ No   2. Do you have a place in your desk, backpack, or locker to keep completed homework?

____ Yes ____ No   3. Do you know how and when your teachers collect homework?

____ Yes ____ No   4. Do you usually turn in your homework on time?

____ Yes ____ No   5. After your homework is returned to you, do you keep it to use at a later time to review for tests?

Category Score_____

Scoring the Inventory and Suggestions to Improve Your Child's Homework Skills

Give your child one point for each check in the "Yes" column and no points for each check in the "No" column of the "Inventory of Homework Skills." Add the scores for each category to obtain a category score. Place each category score next to the appropriate skill. If your child scored four or lower in any category, review the ways your child can improve in that skill.

Skill 1
Writes the assignment given by the teacher and brings home the proper books and supplies.

Your child's category score was: _____

Some students have difficulty recording homework assignments that are given orally in class. They may struggle because their teacher gives assignments at the end of the period when the child may be tired or has not had enough time to write down the assignment accurately. They may not listen carefully when assignments are given, not pay sufficient attention to details (e.g., page numbers, problems to do), and not have sufficient information written to complete the assignment correctly. This can result in a somewhat cryptic description of the homework, which neither you nor they understand. Your child may need a buddy to write down the assignments and give your child a copy or is available to call after school.

It is also important to make certain that your child possess the skill to bring home materials that are necessary to complete homework. There are a number of ways to help your child remember which materials to bring home.

Remembers to Bring Books and Assignments Home

- We suggest that elementary school students divide their desks into two parts (turning in and taking home sides).

- For middle or secondary school students, a place can be set aside on a shelf in their locker for books or other materials during the day that will be needed that evening.

- Some students turn books with the bindings toward the back of the locker to indicate that those books are to go home.

- We are also finding that increasingly schools are providing classrooms with a single set of textbooks that remain in class and are used by different students during the day. The student's personal texts are left at home. Text copies are also in the library for use immediately after school or during the school day, such as in study hall.

- Some students find it easier to carry everything with them to and from school in heavy, but large back packs. This way, nothing is forgotten or lost. Keep in mind, however, that orthopedic experts suggest that your children's back pack should not weigh more than 25 percent of his or her total body weight.

- Some elementary school teachers will provide or allow you to provide a plastic bin your child can keep next to his or her desk all day. A bin is easier to organize and visualize than a desk.

Skill 2
Chooses an appropriate place in which to do homework.

Your child's category score was: _____

Finding a suitable place to do homework can be a challenge. Some children prefer completing homework in the middle of all the action (e.g., at the kitchen or dining room table) and others prefer a quiet location, such as their room. Within these locations children have individual preferences. Some choose to work at a desk, others like to sprawl out on the floor and for some, their bed makes the perfect homework place. If your children are having difficulty with homework, help them find the best place to work. Let them try different places and see how much work they complete. Once a suitable homework place is found, encourage use of that setting, but be flexible as children may prefer different homework places from time to time.

Homework materials—papers, pencils, pens, scissors, notebooks, rulers, a dictionary— should be stored in your homework place. A bright plastic bin or a device such as a materials organizer can help keep all materials in one place. The Homework Helpmate™, made by Sensible Solutions and available through the A.D.D. WareHouse (800-233-9273), would be such an organizer and could be placed next to the Learning Station™.

We also suggest that at the beginning of the school year, you help your child create a resource list or index card file. This list should include names and phone numbers of friends or homework buddies, teachers or homework hotlines, or even helpful Internet addresses.

Skill 3
Starts assignments by reading directions and follow them carefully.

Your child's category score was: _____

Difficulty starting an assignment is a common problem for many children. If this is a problem, we suggest you assist your child by first identifying the primary source of the problem. Is it because the child cannot decide what to begin with, does not understand how to obtain help, does not know how to break tasks into smaller parts, or does not have a consistent routine?

We can help children learn a system to decide which tasks they can do independently and which ones require help. We suggest you have your child work first on those assignments or parts of assignments they can complete independently and successfully. This will establish a pattern of good feelings and success. Help your child decide the order of tasks. They may be done by:

- ✎ Starting with the easiest or the most difficult.

- ✎ Starting with assignments that require out of home resources such as the library.

- ✎ Starting with assignments that appear enjoyable.

- ✎ Doing part of each assignment and finishing or checking it later.

For assignments that require help, we suggest you encourage your child to first try to solve problems on their own. However, if they cannot, encourage them to ask for help. Review a list of people they can use as a resource (parents, siblings, friends, classmates,etc.) or sources they can consult (e.g., dictionary, encyclopedia, map, internet, etc.). Encourage younger children to fill out a "Getting Help Worksheet" so they have a plan for getting needed help independently. A sample worksheet appears below:

Skill 4
Manages difficult
or long-term assignments.

Your child's category score was: _____

Children who score low on this skill will probably need to learn how to manage difficult or long-term assignments. Children are often overwhelmed by multi-step projects or confusing assignments, and their first reaction is to ask for help or put the assignment off for another time. On the following page are some sugges-

tions to teach your child how to handle these types of assignments.

Review your child's assignments to see if there are any long term projects that need to be done. Help your child set up a schedule to do the assignment step-by-step. Children do not intuitively know how to simplify a larger task into manageable steps. To help them with this process, it is useful to focus their attention on the main feature of the task (i.e., the outline, headings, words in italics or bolded, the questions at the end or the beginning of the work). Based on just these general features of complex tasks, ask your child to describe the task or reading material. This strategy helps children reduce large amounts of information to topics, questions, or categories.

There are other ways to reduce information or to make directions easier to understand. For

---

GETTING HELP WORKSHEET

1. What's my question?_____

2. Who will I call?_____

3. What should I do before I call?_____

_____

_____

4. How have I gotten help for this problem in the past?_____

_____

_____

5. Could my parents help me with this problem? _____

From: Seven Steps to Homework Success by S. Zentall and S. Goldstein (Specialty Press, 1999). Limited copies may be made for personal use.

example, children can use magic markers to underline important points in directions or in a reading selection. These important points are often in the first or the topic sentence of a paragraph. Once they can identify the important points, they can use a different colored marker to find the supporting points. This strategy can also be used in listening to teachers' lectures. If note paper were divided into three columns, students could take notes on the main point in column one, supporting points in column two, and questions or thoughts in column three.

Finally, there are ways to reduce the amount of information that must be organized when telling or writing stories. We know that many children will write better stories if they have first drawn small pictures of the story events. One picture can be drawn in each of the squares, created by folding a piece of paper into six to twelve parts.

When children perceive a homework assignment as too difficult, it becomes a self-fulfilling prophecy. The assignment immediately becomes even more difficult because your child perceives it as such. If your child gives up without reasonable effort or requesting help, your child will feel increasingly more helpless and hopeless. Teach your child to question himself: "What do I know?" "What can I do?" and "Who can I ask for help?" Here are some simple suggestions to help your child be active and take control when your child feels an assignment is too difficult.

Handling Difficult Assignments

- ✎ Underline or use magic markers to highlight parts of the directions.

- ✎ Read all of the headings, tables of contents, chapter questions, and bolded words in   reading assignments. Highlight or write them down if that helps. Highlight directions on any

worksheets. If it is a math sheet, highlight symbols and signs.

- ✎ Make lists of important words or concepts.

- ✎ Tell yourself brief summaries into a tape recorder, play them back, and listen carefully. Do they make sense?

- ✎ Tape record answers to questions, such as those written below. Listen back.
    a) What are the advantages and disadvantages of X?
    b) Compare and contrast X and Y.
    c) What was the main point the author was making about X?
    d) What was the sequence of events that lead up to X?
    e) What was the outcome of X?

Skill 5
Maintains attention when assignments are boring.

Your child's category score was: _____

It would be great if everything in life were interesting, but you and your child know that is not the case. Sometimes we just have to work on boring tasks. There are two things you can do to make a dull or boring task more enjoyable:

- Increase the rewards the child will obtain after finishing a dull task. For example, what activities can the child look forward to? What snacks, games, or phone calls will the child make once this task is completed? This is how we all motivate ourselves to complete such tasks.

HOMEWORK PREFERENCES QUESTIONNAIRE

Your Homework Style - Preferences
Check those you prefer. Give examples of preferences.

___Drill and practice   ___Studying for tests   ___Reports

• Projects. What kinds do you like?

1._____   3. _____

2._____   4._____

• Outside of classroom assignments. What kinds do you like?

1._____

2._____

• Change a boring task into something that is more interesting or into a game. Encourage your child to be creative. Play beat the clock, etc.

What kind of homework does your child prefer doing? What is your child's favorite and least favorite activity? The "Homework Preferences Questionnaire" above will help children develop a better understanding of the kinds of homework they enjoys most and those assignments that may be more difficult to complete. We suggest that you and your child complete the questionnaire and discuss your child's interests and preferences. This may also be good information for your child's teacher to have.

Skill 6
Checks work for accuracy and thoroughness.

Your child's category score was: _____

Most children rush through their homework. It is important to help your children develop habits to check their work. In an effort to reduce boredom, we suggest that children move on to another assignment and then return at a later point to check previous assignments. It is also time efficient for children to have checklists they can cross off to make certain that essential steps for an assignment are completed. A sample story writing checklist appears above.

Additionally, if your children write out answers to math problems, they could read a few aloud or use a calculator as a checker. Or your child could use finger puppets to check work.

STORY WRITING CHECKLIST

HAVE I CHECKED:

____ Yes ____ No   Name and date?

____ Yes ____ No   Main points as topic sentences?

____ Yes ____ No   Summary sections?

____ Yes ____ No   Conclusion section?

____ Yes ____ No   Spelling on the computer?

____ Yes ____ No   References section?

From: Seven Steps to Hassle-Free Homework by S. Zentall and S. Goldstein (Specialty Press, 1999). Limited copies may be made for personal use.

We knew a student named Brad who drew a face on the fist of his hand, with eyes on his index finger and a mouth across his thumb. He named his hand puppet Jack. Jack's job was to check Brad's work and tell him to correct certain parts of it. Brad, of course, protested at having to make these corrections, but did them anyway. Brad watched while Jack looked for mistakes, and Jack watched, while Brad made the corrections.

Skill 7
Returns homework
to school when it is due.

Your child's category score was: _____

Some children have not learned the skill of preparing their work to hand in to the teacher. They may have completed homework at home, but they either forget to bring the assignment to school, misplace it, or miss the teacher's instruc-tions to turn it in. Children who forget to bring homework from home to school should first try keeping a homework folder in their back pack. When homework is finished each night, children should get in the habit of putting it in the folder. Parents may need to remind the child in the morning to look over assignments due that day and check to make certain they are packed away for school.

Another way to help your child remember to turn in homework is to create an assignment tracking sheet such as the one on the previous page. The child should mark when assignments in each subject are due and whether the textbook, notebook, or worksheets need to be brought to school the next day.

HOMEWORK TRACKING SHEET

Monday

Time Period	Subject	Assignment	Due	Text	Notebook	Worksheet
	English					
	Science					
	Math					
	Social Studies					
	Social Science					

Tuesday

Time Period	Subject	Assignment	Due	Text	Notebook	Worksheet
	English					
	Science					
	Math					
	Social Studies					
	Social Science					

Wednesday

Time Period	Subject	Assignment	Due	Text	Notebook	Worksheet
	English					
	Science					
	Math					
	Social Studies					
	Social Science					

Thursday

Time Period	Subject	Assignment	Due	Text	Notebook	Worksheet
	English					
	Science					
	Math					
	Social Studies					
	Social Science					

Friday

Time Period	Subject	Assignment	Due	Text	Notebook	Worksheet
	English					
	Science					
	Math					
	Social Studies					
	Social Science					

Summary

In this step we have identified seven essential homework skills your child must learn and practice to be able to manage homework independently. Your child completed the "Inventory of Homework Skills" to determine areas of strength and weakness. We provided suggestions to help your child improve in any of the seven areas where skill weakness was evident.

Now it is time to move on to step three—Developing a Homework Alliance with Your Child. This step discusses the important role parents play in helping children learn homework skills and in teaching them to be responsible for their school work. You will evaluate your role as a parent as it pertains to school and homework.

STEP 3
Developing a Homework Alliance with Your Child

Step 3
Developing a Homework Alliance with Your Child

Parents who are involved in helping their child with homework know it is a team effort. In the best of situations, the child works independently and the parent stands by ready to provide assistance and feedback when necessary. Not all parents have the time or ability to provide the help their child may need with homework. In this step we will help you examine your role as a parent member of this homework team and provide you with a variety of ways you can encourage your child's education. These guidelines will help you and your child develop a productive homework alliance.

In step two we identified seven essential skills children must learn to be able to manage homework independently. Children must be able to:

1. Record the assignment given by the teacher and bring home the proper books and supplies.

2. Choose an appropriate place in which to complete homework.

3. Start assignments by reading directions and follow them carefully.

4. Manage difficult or long-term assignments.

5. Maintain attention when assignments are boring.

6. Check work to make certain it is accurate and thorough.

7. Return homework to school and turn it in when it is due.

In this step we have identified 25 parent practices, which can have a very positive role in shaping how your child learns to manage homework. These practices address broad issues such as parent involvement in school, parent-teacher communication, parental supervision of child behavior, establishment and enforcement of homework routines, value placed on education in the home, and willingness to provide assistance to your child with homework.

On the following pages is the "Positive Parent Homework Practices" questionnaire, which we suggest you complete. Your answers will give you a good idea of your strengths and weaknesses regarding homework assistance.

POSITIVE PARENT HOMEWORK PRACTICES

Name of Parent _____   Date _____

____ Yes ____ No	1.	Do you volunteer time to your child's classroom or school?
____ Yes ____ No	2.	Do you go to school conferences or meetings about your child?
____ Yes ____ No	3.	Do you ask the teacher about your child's homework practices and policies?
____ Yes ____ No	4.	Are you aware of your child's whereabouts after school?
____ Yes ____ No	5.	Do you monitor your child's homework after school or by using a trusted individual or tutor?
____ Yes ____ No	6.	Do you monitor your child's homework after school with a written or taped list and with a phone call?
____ Yes ____ No	7.	Do you or your child have homework times established?
____ Yes ____ No	8.	Does your child follow these times and do you enforce these homework times?
____ Yes ____ No	9.	Do you limit TV time or make sure it is given after your child has worked on homework?
____ Yes ____ No	10.	Have you helped your child experiment with different places to study and different home conditions (with music/TV on, at a desk, on the bed, etc.)?
____ Yes ____ No	11.	Do you provide healthy homework snacks for your child after school?
____ Yes ____ No	12.	Have you helped your child identify activities or breaks that are rewards for completing a certain amount of homework?
____ Yes ____ No	13.	Does your child have or have you helped your child develop a way to plan for a long-term project, with checks and reminders?
____ Yes ____ No	14	Do you ask about what your child learned at school that day and about his/her interests?
____ Yes ____ No	15.	Does your child have a system of putting homework in a specific place?
____ Yes ____ No	16.	Do you help your child practice skills using games or flashcards?
____ Yes ____ No	17.	Do you help your child understand directions by asking your child what he/she reads?
____ Yes ____ No	18.	Do you allow the child an alternative way to demonstrate what he/she knows (e.g., drawing pictures when typing, talking)?
____ Yes ____ No	19.	Do you read to your child when the objective of the lesson is not reading but understanding the content (e.g., social studies, math problem solving)?
____ Yes ____ No	20.	Do you provide ways to make homework faster or more fun (colorful folders, pencils, organizers, choice, getting them started, positive statements)?

____ Yes ____ No   21. Do you provide tape recorded messages, check sheets, tours of the public library, references, choice, and goal setting to develop independence?

____ Yes ____ No   22. Do you help your child prioritize homework tasks?

____ Yes ____ No   23. Would you hire a tutor if your child's skill level is significantly below the homework requirements?

____ Yes ____ No   24. Do you find ways to praise your child for good work and homework?

____ Yes ____ No   25. Do you help your child study for tests by quizzing your child on material to be learned?

Once you have completed this questionnaire, review the questions you responded to with "No." Think about how your child may benefit if you were to modify your behavior in these areas. Would you be more involved in your child's education? Would you establish and enforce more homework routines? Would you provide more assistance to your child if help and feedback were needed with respect to homework? Would your child value education more as a result of your example and instruction?

---

15 Guidelines to Create a Homework Alliance with Your Child

Below are 15 guidelines to help you work with your child to manage homework.

#1 Stay Involved with Homework and Monitor After School Activities

Your involvement will help you and your child begin to build a homework alliance. As a member of this homework team, you will need to work hard to encourage your child's school work. You may need to listen to your child read, participate in learning games or story telling, and make yourself available as needed. All of these activities have been reported to increase elementary students' achievement, with the greatest gains in reading skills. Your positive involvement will increase homework completion, school attendance, improve your child's attitude toward school, and decrease the likelihood your child will experience behavioral problems in school.[1]

Many demands placed on families today make it difficult for parents to schedule the time necessary to be involved on a daily basis. Teachers often complain that it is difficult for them to involve parents actively with children's homework. It is unclear whether this is the result of parents being too busy, not understanding the assigned work, or simply uncertain of their role in the homework process. In most cases, it is not the result of disinterest. However, be assured that whatever problems arise, there are many different ways you can establish an effective homework alliance. Take a moment and answer the questions on the following page.

MONITORING AFTER SCHOOL ACTIVITIES

____ Yes ____ No   1. Are you at home when your child returns from school?

____ Yes ____ No   2. Is your child with a trusted friend or adult relative after school if you are not available?

____ Yes ____ No   3. Is your child tutored after school?

____ Yes ____ No   4. Does a written or taped list of instructions or activities await your child's return home from school?

____ Yes ____ No   5. Is there a consistent, daily routine followed after school?

____ Yes ____ No   6. If you are not home, do you phone your child or have your child phone you after school?

____ Yes ____ No   7. Do you or the child have a pager or cell phone to promote communication?

____ Yes ____ No   8. Is there a message center in your house (bulletin board, etc.) where you and your child write notes when there are changes in routines?

____ Yes ____ No   9. Does a trusted friend or neighbor, adult relative, or older sibling check on your child after school?

If you answered "No" to five or more of these questions, it will be important for you to address these issues. You may need to improve monitoring of after school activities, particularly for children under the age of 12.

There are many things you can do to increase the chances that your child will successfully complete homework. Parental involvement can mean just knowing where your child is after school or supervising after school performance. These types of monitoring were found to relate to the number of hours children devoted to homework[2].

2 Provide Options and Choice in Work Space

The way you structure home conditions (e.g., place for homework, noise, light, television, availability of resources) has been found to play an important role in predicting homework performance. In fact, these issues have been found to be even more important than checking and signing homework. Consider experimenting with a variety of locations and noise levels to decide what works best for your child. A quiet, isolated setting is not necessarily the best for everyone. It may surprise you to learn that children can complete homework and perform well in a variety of positions and places. Remember homework is not like medicine. It does not have to taste bad to be good for you. In fact, the more pleasant you can make the surrounding study conditions, schedules, and materials, the more likely your child will approach homework positively.

Settings are best selected by your child because optimal conditions may change as your child's age, abilities, and assignments change. Allow your child some decision making power in trying out different places for different tasks. The portable Learning Station™ (which we will show you how to build in step five) helps set the stage for effective homework conditions and assists in organizing and tracking materials.

HOMEWORK PREFERENCE DIARY

How does your child perform homework assignments in these places in the presence of television, music, or silence? After trying a location out for a few days, rate it on a scale of 1-4 as follows: 1 = great; 2 = good; 3 = okay; 4 = poor. Try varying conditions as well.

	CONDITIONS		
LOCATIONS	**Television**	**Music**	**Silence**
Kitchen Table	1 2 3 4	1 2 3 4	1 2 3 4
Bedroom - on bed	1 2 3 4	1 2 3 4	1 2 3 4
Bedroom - on floor	1 2 3 4	1 2 3 4	1 2 3 4
Bedroom - on desk	1 2 3 4	1 2 3 4	1 2 3 4
Dining room table	1 2 3 4	1 2 3 4	1 2 3 4
Family room on floor	1 2 3 4	1 2 3 4	1 2 3 4
Family room on couch	1 2 3 4	1 2 3 4	1 2 3 4
Other _____	1 2 3 4	1 2 3 4	1 2 3 4

Which setting, under which condition, with which type of assignments works best for your child?

_____

_____

_____

How and where does your child complete homework best? We suggest you create an experiment to discover this process. By completing the following diary, you can evaluate the time and place that is best for your child.

Junior high school students are more likely to complete homework in the presence of music and less likely to do so without it.[3] The impact of music during repetitive tasks may be even more important for students with Attention-deficit/Hyperactivity Disorder (ADHD), who perform better with music than with silence or with speech in the background.[4] Some children with ADHD, especially if they are older or without learning problems, can even work with television in the background. This is probably true of all children during the performance of many tasks. Once you and your child have identified the best conditions for different types of homework, you are ready to plan a daily schedule.

3 Establish A Family Routine of Talking About the Value of Learning

Another simple type of involvement is to discuss learning at the dinner table. Children will understand that education and learning are valued. For example, each child can take turns talking about what was learned that day at school. You can talk about work experiences and current events. These discussions might also involve problems or conflicts that were encountered, solutions that were chosen, and questions that remain. Such discussions communicate that effort, interests, and even making mistakes are vital in the process of learning and growing. The encouragement of interests will be significant in moving your child toward independence—and can be more important in the long term than the specific grades your child receives. One way for you to assess children's interests is to have them put together a scrapbook or collage related to an interest, collection, or preferred foods or activities.

4 Plan a Daily Schedule

It is important to set a family rule for homework times, such as "Homework must be done between 5 p.m. and 6 p.m." Homework times should not be assigned late in the evening nor when you are aware your child is tired. Enforcing time schedules for homework is an effective way of increasing the number of assignments completed.[5] However, when you do not monitor the time schedule, you may discover that your child will not maintain the schedule independently. Therefore, it is important for you to consistently reinforce this schedule as a family rule. A behavior needs to be repeated many, many times before it becomes a habit or routine. More repetitions will be needed for younger children or for children with learning disabilities. For children with ADHD, there is greater difficulty with, and therefore resistance to, repeating behavior patterns and establishing habits. Thus, all of these children in particular will require encouragement, choice, and/or rewards to develop consistent homework habits.

If homework is to be completed immediately after a snack or play time, but before preferred activities (e.g., television) enforce this rule consistently. A daily plan can be communicated to your child by a written or tape recorded list of activities, specifying times to be spent on homework, chores, or preferred activities. We suggest you consider a number of short homework periods in the early afternoon interspersed with preferred activity times, especially for children with attentional deficits or learning disabilities. The Learning Station™ (discussed in step five) offers an ideal way to accomplish this goal.

You should develop a list of preferred activities with your child. These can be available when homework is completed. You can have your child design his or her own "TV Guide" of favorite programs for the month. With this schedule, preferred activities can be added just like the programs on television. With a bit of creativity, even chores can be entertaining.

Television programs can also be taped and provided to your child in 15 minute blocks of time (i.e. 15 minutes of work equals 15 minutes of a preferred television program). Rewards such as additional time prior to bedtime, have been used to increase the number of minutes working on homework.[6] Certain snacks might also be made available only during homework time. Family outings or special family conversation time might also be offered as rewards for homework completion.

Try not to deny access to an activity that may be an important "one-time" event (e.g., the circus coming to town, the birthday party of a good friend or relative).

Make certain that you spend a fixed amount of time with your child each week that is not dependent upon the quality of their behavior or work. Make sure your child has access to sports and recreational activities that are also not dependent upon the quality of behavior or homework. Below is a list of preferred activities to begin this process. We suggest you add your own ideas with input from your child.

ELEMENTARY AGE PREFERRED ACTIVITIES TO EARN

Daily

1. Play a game with parents or sibling.
2. Cook a snack with parent for school or for child.
3. Stay up 30 minutes later or watch TV 30 minutes of extra time.
4. Read comics or work on a model.
5. Receive money to be saved.
6. Choose dinner or dessert menu.
7. Sit in front seat of car.
8. Play outside longer.
9. Play with a special toy.
10. _____

Weekly

1. Invite a friend or friends overnight or to a party.
2. Invite a friend or friends to do an activity.
3. Special activities with parents such as bowling, playing basketball, movies, etc.
4. Have a picnic in the park.
5. Buy some seeds to plant.
6. Rearrange or redecorate bedroom.
7. _____

SECONDARY AGE PREFERRED ACTIVITIES TO EARN

Daily

1. Stay out or up later.
2. Earn money toward a desired object or activity.
3. Play video games or rent videos to watch at home on the VCR.
4. Choice of TV programs on certain nights.
5. Spend time with parent on project (e.g., science, fixing car).
6. Have a friend or friends over after school with a snack provided.
7. _____

Weekly

1. Use of family car or driven to places if not of driving age.
2. Receive tickets to special events (e.g., rock concerts, sports).
3. Invite friends to special events or with family to a restaurant.
4. Receive CDs or tapes.
5. Receive coupons for TV programs
6. _____
7. _____

On the following page are two worksheets. The first, "Homework Completion Leading to Preferred Activities," will help you connect homework to rewards. It is always best to use a positive rather than a negative approach to homework motivation. The second one demonstrates how such a worksheet might look after your child has it completed and set up for the week.

HOMEWORK COMPLETION LEADING TO PREFERRED ACTIVITIES

Weekly Chores, Days, and Time (e.g., take out trash on Wednesday-takes 10 minutes)

_____

_____

_____

Assignments: Circle the subject areas for which you have assignments each week:

Reading/English   Social Studies   Science   Spelling   Other

Select a way to assess progress on assignments from A or B:

A.   How much **time** on an assignment?_____

B.   How many:
        (1) pages   _____
        (2) problems   _____
        (3) assignments   _____

My choices will follow Chores and Assignments (A or B above):

1. Preferred activities, day, and time (Example: Boy Scouts on Tuesdays for 60
   minutes).

_____

_____

2. TV programs and time blocks.

_____

_____

GOALS FOR MY HOMEWORK AND MY ACTIVITIES

FOR THE WEEK OF: _____

EXAMPLE:

MONDAY: 4 p.m.: reading =30 minutes with snack

               Followed by computer game = 10 minutes

               Math problems on pages 75-77

               Followed by play with dog = 10 minutes

               Mow lawn = 30 minutes

               Followed by television = 1 hour

TUESDAY   _____

               _____

               _____

               _____

               _____

WEDNESDAY   _____

               _____

               _____

               _____

               _____

THURSDAY   _____

               _____

               _____

               _____

               _____

FRIDAY   _____

               _____

               _____

               _____

               _____

5 Plan Ahead

Children do not necessarily do what we say; they often do as we do. In order for your children to learn how to prioritize, organize, and plan for daily and longer assignments, you must be available to model and teach them an effective system. A simple calendar like the one below is a good start.

You can use this calendar to help your child keep track of upcoming tests, quizzes, reports, and even daily assignments if they are offered at the beginning of the week. Use the calendar to break long-term projects into shorter steps. Reproducing this schedule on a dry erase board can allow you to easily make adjustments as needed.

6 Provide Assistance

The amount of assistance your child needs will be determined by his or her age and level of ability. Young students as well as those with learning problems require more of your time, assistance, and support. Your assistance also depends on whether the homework assignments represent practicing a skill already mastered by your child or developing and mastering a new skill.

It is also likely that you will feel more competent helping your child with certain types of homework tasks. For example, fathers often feel more comfortable helping with math and mothers feel more comfortable with language arts. When both parents are available in a two-parent home, we advise that they both assist with homework. In one-parent homes, tutors may be helpful.

Furthermore, as we have discussed, most parents feel quite capable of providing assistance when the goal of homework is to practice previously learned information. For example, using flash cards and helping children develop reading vocabulary represents such an activity. This procedure typically involves having your child write individual reading words on separate index cards. It is often best to start with a few cards containing high-interest words and a num-

PROJECT SCHEDULE

MONTH OF _____ (enter dates)

Sat.	Sun.	Mon.	Tues.	Wed.	Thur.	Fri.

ber of words your child reads well. Then hold up one card at a time from the stack, and your child will read each word. When the word is read correctly, your child keeps the card. When your child misses the word you say, "The correct word is _____." Ask your child to restate the correct word, but keep that card and place it under the stack. This procedure can be repeated each evening. Add new words and give your child those that are quickly identified.

In contrast, you may feel less capable assisting your child when new skills or problem solving exercises have been assigned. When acquiring new information is the object of a homework lesson, it may be important for you to ask questions about the materials, to summarize for your child any past strengths in that area, or to ask how you can be of assistance.

#7 Develop a System for Returning Homework to School

Make sure your child is returning homework to school. This goal can be accomplished by having a specific place in your child's backpack and in the house that homework is placed each evening. Your child can select one or two places

to store the backpack. Baskets or boxes with pictures of the backpack can be placed in these locations. We also suggest a folder for homework and your assistance in making certain that the folder stays in your child's backpack. It is critical that your child's teacher checks the folder each day. With the increasing use of technology, homework can be faxed or e-mailed to school. The Internet may be used to access the teacher's online files. Parents can check these files for their child's completed work.

#8 Adapt Assignments to Maximize Your Child's Strengths

If your child is a poor reader and the purpose of a social studies assignment is to learn about a specific time in history, forcing your child to struggle through reading the material is not productive. This could lead to a dislike of both reading and history. In other words, do not allow your child's skill weaknesses to interfere when the purpose of an assignment is gaining knowledge. If your child experiences problems with reading or reading speed, either read the material to or with your child. These compensations will allow your child to focus on understanding and comprehending the material.

In contrast, when increasing reading speed and proficiency is the goal of a homework assignment, then your child must read independently. Children at all ability levels, when asked to read out loud to their parents, improve reading skills above and beyond children who do not have this reading experience.

#9 Do not Change Lesson Objectives

If the lesson objective is solving math story problems, then reading the problems to your child or allowing your child to use a calculator does not represent a change of lesson objective. However, if the objective is math calculation and your child computes math problems using a calculator, then a change of lesson objective has been made. In this case, allowing your child to check math calculations with a calculator could be used as a reinforcer after a certain number of problems are completed. Such an activity would not involve changing the lesson objective.

The lesson objective may not always be apparent. If you are familiar with a subject area (e.g., reading, math, social studies), then you may have an idea of the general content objective. If you read the instructions provided to your child, you can probably figure out what skills the assignment is targeting. You can assess your ability to figure out assignment objectives using the examples on the following page. Correct answers are listed at the end of this quiz.

How did you do? If your answers were correct, you can be generally confident you will be able to quickly understand and discern the objectives of your child's homework. However, if a number of your answers were incorrect, we suggest you take the time to strengthen your skills in this area. One way to begin this process is to communicate with your child's teacher to make certain that you understand the assigned objectives of the homework.

#10 Help Your Child Use Strengths to Demonstrate Knowledge

It may also be important for you to alter the way your child demonstrates knowledge. If the

lesson objective is understanding what was read or heard, demonstration of this objective might involve: (a) drawing a sequence of cartoons to show the story events; (b) verbally describing or typing the sequence of events; or (c) play acting out the events. All of these would represent valid yet different ways of demonstrating what was learned. However, if your child's teacher is working on constructing stories, then a change of objective would occur if you allowed your child to draw a series of cartoons. Verbally describing or typing the story events, however, would not be a change in the lesson objective.

#11 Do Not Do Homework for Your Child

Even though you may make an assignment easier by altering the assignment or responses to that assignment, rarely, if ever, should you complete the homework yourself. It is better for your child to do just part of an assignment well than to do none of it. When parents complete homework, children rarely benefit. Here are several additional suggestions if you are unsure about how to provide positive assistance without directly doing the work for your child.

1. Help your child get started.

2. Help your child prioritize the specific tasks to be done.

3. Make certain your child understands the directions for each assignment.

4. Provide your child with magic markers to highlight important information.

5. Provide incentives (e.g., preferred activities when each task is completed.).

When interviewed about their homework practices, parents of elementary level boys with

ASSIGNMENT OBJECTIVES QUIZ FOR PARENTS

Read the following questions and circle the correct answer.

1. Read about Brazil and answer the questions about the geography and political history of this country. This a question that targets:

   (a) reading
   (b) understanding the culture

2. Write an editorial for a Brazilian newspaper and decide whether you will support or oppose the cutting of tropical forests in Brazil. This a question that targets:

   (a) handwriting
   (b) composing a story

3. Rewrite these sentences, using commas. This a direction that requires:

   (a) knowledge of punctuation rules
   (b) handwriting

4. Read pages 10-20 and define the terms "erosion" and "weathering." This a direction that requires:

   (a) prior vocabulary knowledge
   (b) reading for understanding

5. Based on what you learned in class today, read the following paragraph and write down all the reasons for why this location is a good site for a city. This a direction that requires:

   (a) application of knowledge
   (b) reading for understanding

6. The child is to read to learn about exports of a country and has difficulty with specific words or misreads specific words. What would you do?

   (a) stop the child to "sound out" or "look up" those words
   (b) tell the child the words

Answers to objective quiz (1 = b; 2 = b; 3 = a; 4 = b; 5 = a; 6 = b)

ADHD (with and without giftedness) reported specific kinds of help they gave that did not involve changing assignment objectives.[7] For example, mothers reported a wide variety of techniques (e.g., reading or writing for their children, giving them activity breaks between assignments, using incentives, choice, and discussions). Mothers also reported communicating with the teacher (e.g., to get assignments shortened). Fathers reported giving their child attention, getting them started, and showing them how to figure things out.

One of our favorite techniques is to request that your child be the teacher and teach you about the assignment while you pretend to be the child. It is well recognized that we all learn more when we teach what we have learned to someone else. This process will also indicate how well your child has mastered the material by the ways in which he/she teaches it to you.

12 Use Outside Resources

If your child does not want help with homework but clearly needs it, agree in advance who will provide assistance. It could be you, one of your other children or even a neighbor. In some cases you may wish to hire a tutor, especially if your child has a specific learning disability or an emotional or behavioral problem. Keep in mind that part of the process in establishing a homework alliance is to also build and reinforce a positive relationship with your child. For this purpose and at this time, you may not want to assist with homework. In addition to providing a tutor, there are a number of available books that explain how to teach your child essential organizational and school survival skills, including note taking and studying. One such book for middle and high school students is "Study Strategies Made Easy" (A.D.D. WareHouse 800-233-9273).

13 Avoid Excessive Correction

Excessive correction reduces everyone's motivation and increases feelings of low self-worth. Be sensitive when providing feedback. Learning occurs in safe environments where children do not need to defend their actions, strate-

---

WORDS OF ENCOURAGEMENT

- You are really improving.
- You must be proud of this.
- You made a good choice.
- I'm very proud of you.
- Show me how.
- I like that.
- This is the best yet.
- I like the way you do that.

- That's interesting.
- Yes, I've never thought of it that way.
- Tell me more.
- You are really sticking with it.
- I love the way you can _____.
- That was very thoughtful.
- You are doing fine.

gies, or opinions. Correction is necessary for children to learn what does not work or is inefficient. Most times, however, children will arrive at their own understanding. This process can be accelerated by asking children if they can think of another way to complete the task. You can guide children specifically if you ask them to think of a faster, more careful way, or a way that a tricky fox would use, etc.

However, when accuracy is important and there is only one correct answer or response, you can look for similarities in mistakes and point out mistakes as a group. Alternately you can point out a single mistake and ask your child to find others of the same type and fix them all at one time (one error rather than many). Children also learn well from general rules to prevent errors.

Remember that your child will learn best when you point out what is correct and what is better than the last time. This is particularly true of children who have suffered from "success deprivation" at school. A good rule is to provide at least three compliments for every correction. In general, praising effort is better and more realistic than falsely claiming the work as a whole is outstanding. Keep in mind that your child may compare his or her work to others. For this reason, you should encourage comparisons of your child's work with his or her previous work and

THE ANIMALS AT SCHOOL STORY[8]

Once upon a time, the animals decided they must do something heroic to meet the problems of "a new world," so they organized a school. They adopted an activity curriculum consisting of running, climbing, swimming, and flying. To make it easier to implement, all the animals took all the subjects.

The duck was excellent in swimming, better than his instructor, and made passing grades in flying, but he was very poor in running. Since he was slow in running, he had to stay after school and also drop swimming to practice running. This continued until his webbed feet were badly worn, and he was only average in swimming. But average was acceptable in school, so nobody worried about that except the duck.

The rabbit started at the top of the class in running, but had a nervous breakdown because of so much make-up work for swimming.

The squirrel was excellent in climbing until he became frustrated in the flying class. His teacher made him start from the ground-up instead of from the tree-top-down. He also developed a charlie horse from over-exertion, he got a C in climbing and a D in running.

The eagle was a problem child and was disciplined severely. In the climbing class he beat all the others to the top of the tree, but insisted on using his own way to get there.

At the end of the year, an abnormal eel that could swim exceedingly well, run, climb, and fly a little held the highest average and was valedictorian.

The prairie dogs stayed out of school and fought the tax levy because the administration would not add digging and burrowing to the curriculum. They apprenticed their children to a badger and later joined the groundhogs and gophers to start a successful private school.[7]

effort—not with others. These self-comparisons will improve long-term motivation. In the box below are some words of encouragement you might say.

Listen carefully to what your child has to say about homework and be sensitive to any feelings of frustration or pleasure as a result of success. It is important for you to view homework and education within the total fabric of your child's life. Education requires children to be generalists, who are good at everything. But life requires adults to specialize and demonstrate perseverance. Thus, there are only a few things that require real interest or skill. Adults can hire others to help them with their weak areas (e.g., filling out tax returns). They can work on teams with others who may possess different skills. The tale in the box, "The Animals at School Story," communicates some of the artificiality of many school environments. Consider the moral of this story. What can you do to make school more meaningful in your child's life?

14 Remain Task Oriented

It is important for you to accept the feelings of frustration your child may have when dealing with homework. Redirect him or her back to the current task; explain what needs to be done and how to best do it. It is okay for your child to feel frustrated. This is important information for you; it indicates that there is a problem to be solved. In response, if you become irritable or angry, this will only heighten your anxiety as well as your child's frustration. Perhaps a good initial question to ask your child is "In what ways do you want help?" The following suggestions are additional ways to deal with homework in different subjects.

Reading
- Read topic sentences.
- Read headings.
- Read questions at the end.
- Teach the SQ3R technique to review content material.[9] SQ3R stands for Scan, Question, Read, Recite, and Review. Scanning requires a survey of the material, including pictures, featured key words, and a summary. Questioning means turning each bold faced heading and word into a question. After reading the material thoroughly, bold faced type should be recited out loud. Finally, key words and questions raised from bold faced titles should be reviewed.
- Worksheets and workbooks should be divided into fragments or chunks. Encourage your child to work on one chunk at a time.
- Have your child work with a friend and read out loud, taking turns as homework is completed.
- Present key vocabulary words in a sentence format when they are introduced. This may give immediate meaning to an unknown word.
- Allow your child to select high interest material for reading reports and projects.
- Encourage your child to orally discuss what they have read and even use a tape recorder to record highlights.

Math
- Use calculators to check computations.
- Estimate answers before computing the problem.
- Use color codes when math symbols are changed on worksheets. For example, make plus signs green and minus signs red.
- Encourage your child to use one inch graph paper to help organize columns.
- Consider novel math strategies such as a math rap tape (Pace, Inc., 7803 Pickering Street, Kalamazoo, Michigan 49022; SRA Technology Train-

ing Company, 155 North Wacker Drive, Chicago, Illinois 60606) to increase interest and exert necessary effort when memorizing math facts.

- Use real life examples, visual models, and manipulatives as often as possible.
- Try mnemonic strategies to help students remember multiple steps and math problems.
- Computers and interesting software should also be considered for tedious math review and drill.

Spelling

- Encourage the use of a computer as a compensatory strategy for spelling and grammar.
- Provide lists of most frequently misspelled words.
- Provide lists of homonyms (e.g., their - there)
- Make use of coloring specific letter combinations that appear difficult for the child to remember.
- Encourage the use of manipulatives when studying for spelling tests, such as letter tiles and magnetic letters.

Story Writing

- Have your child draw small sketches of the sequence of events or ideas of the story that will be written.

Writing

- Break writing assignments down into parts or chapters that you can check.

A LATCH KEY CHILD BECOMES SUCCESSFUL WITH HOMEWORK AND THEN BECOMES A LAWYER

A story was told to us about a latch-key child, who had great difficulty organizing herself after school in her parents' absence.

Her parents first tried placing post-it-notes around the house to remind her of after school homework tasks, chores, and snacks. These techniques, whether in the form of lists or pictures, did not seem to have any effect.

One day the mother remembered the child had a favorite song, which she was always listening to. So with this germ of an idea, the mother made a tape that began with the favorite song and proceeded with several instructions and ended with the rest of the song. With this simple monitoring and guiding device, the child would race home to hear her personal tape and favorite song, which had been recorded by each parent.

The question remained for us about whether the use of this "crutch" indicated that the child would ever be able to run with it. And in asking this question of the story-teller, we were told that the child is now an adult and a beginning lawyer. The "crutch" has helped her with her roommate, who leaves her taped messages and with her secretary, who takes and leaves taped messages. Essentially this child became a very successful adult whose life was organized around this simple homework adaptation. In other words, she now runs faster than most people with her crutch.

- If your child experiences significant written language problems, consider acting as a secretary or working with your child's teacher to allow tape recorded reports to accompany written products.

Homework can also play an important role in helping you understand your child's learning style. Watch your child as homework is being completed. Provide feedback and ask your child's opinion about what appears to work best. Avoid non-productive comments such as "You will never go to college if you do not learn to read" or "You're just like me, I couldn't understand math either." Such comments shift the focus from the task to your child's self-worth. Although misery may love company, it is unlikely that telling your child that you struggled in math will make your child feel better. It would be better for you to say, "You seem to be able to answer more chapter questions when you look at all the picture captions, charts, graphs, and subtitles before reading" or "Let's make a list of the steps to follow when doing these math problems." Such comments provide children with a direction to accomplish tasks by using strengths rather than motivating them with parental fears.[10]

15 Help Your Child Gain Independence

Eventually it will be important to transfer adult assistance to methods that will improve self-help for your child with homework. Remember that an important goal of homework is to develop independence and responsibility. Thus, the most important lesson to be learned from homework is how to complete it successfully the next time. Fostering independence is accomplished by moving your child from dependence on you to dependence on homework buddies and material resources (e.g., references, lists, taped reminders). Remember that focusing on what is right about your child is the best way to help him or her strengthen and develop homework completion skills.

Although young children require your close observation, support, and your ability to identify their work style and preferences, eventually you must provide your child with opportunities for decision making, planning, and goal setting. This is particularly important to achieve prior to the adolescent years when there is a more delicate balance between assistance and interference. During the adolescent years, your teen may prefer to complete work alone, and your assistance may be perceived as an intrusion. It may be unwelcome. By the middle school years, homework should be completed independently. You should act as a consultant and information source rather than a task master or supervisor. Forcing your assistance on your young teen will only result in conflict and reduced motivation. Particularly at this age your involvement may be most effective when it is defined as awareness and monitoring rather than direct assistance or physical supervision.

Summary

We first introduced you to 25 positive parenting practices, which can help your child succeed in school and improve homework completion. Parents who are involved with their child's school work can develop a homework alliance with their child. While it is your child's responsibility to complete homework independently, you must play an important advisory role and should be prepared to provide assistance when needed.

We then discussed 15 guidelines to help you define the role parents should play in the homework process. We have provided a number of strategies and worksheets that you can implement with your child.

Now it is time to move on to step four—11 Common Homework Problems and How to Solve Them. Parents and children often develop patterns of behavior around homework that are nonproductive and cause additional stress. In step four we have identified several of these common homework problems and offer you solutions.

STEP 4
11 Common Homework
Problems and How to Solve Them

Step 4
11 Common Homework
Problems and How to Solve Them

In this chapter we identified 11 common homework problems. Your ability as a parent to recognize these problems and to implement recommended solutions will help you reach the goal of homework success.

Some of these problems may exist because your child needs to practice some of the homework skills that were discussed in step two. Some children may have difficulty learning, behaving, or paying attention, which makes it harder for them to apply these homework skills. We will discuss how you can help if your child experiences any of these problems.

Other difficulties arise when parents don't practice the positive homework behaviors we discussed in step three.

You and your child may have gotten into the habit of interacting with one another in ways that are nonproductive. These nonproductive patterns of interaction often develop into behavioral habits that can be difficult to recognize and change.

Look over the list of 11 common homework problems. See if you can recognize any of them in your family.

11 Common Homework Problems

1. When your child won't do homework without you.
2. When your child repeatedly makes excuses to avoid doing homework.
3. When your child doesn't understand homework.
4. When your child waits until the last minute to do homework .
5. When your child takes too long to complete homework.
6. When your child rushes through homework and makes errors.
7. When your child lacks confidence to do homework independently.
8. When your child complains that homework is boring.
9. When your child has a learning disability.
10. When your child has an attention-deficit/hyperactivity disorder (ADHD).
11. When your child is struggling with emotions, behavior, or development.

When Your Child Won't Do Homework Without You

Do your palms start to sweat when you ask your child about homework, knowing that the answer to this seemingly harmless question might start World War III in your home? Some parents try to avoid the question as long as they can, hoping to have a few more hours of peace until the nightly homework battles begin. Others tackle the problem head-on and ask the question practically before the child has both feet through the door. Some parents may not get involved enough in their child's homework. Others may get too involved, causing the child to become overly reliant on the parent for homework assistance.

It seems clear to us that as a parent you must be involved in your child's learning. You have the responsibility to make sure your child is getting the best education possible and that your child is taking school seriously. To know that, you have to be involved in your child's school work. Parental involvement in your child's education is extremely important if you want your child to succeed in school. Parents who are uninvolved, who do not ask about school, who do not check assignments, who do not go to parent-teacher meetings or communicate with the school are likely to have children who are less successful learners. Parental follow-up about homework is also one of the ways in which you support your child's teachers.

BUILDING INDEPENDENCE

How many trials does it take for your child to learn a skill? How often must they engage in and successfully complete homework independently before they develop the skills and motivation necessary to do so on a daily basis?

Consider two children—Michael and Elliott. During his first grade year, with support from his parents, Michael developed the skills necessary to complete homework independently. When he was uncertain of a task or homework activity, he would seek help from his parents but would then return to independent work. On the other hand, Elliott started out similar to Michael but needed more help and appeared to be less certain of his skills and abilities. His parents, in an effort to make certain that he did not fail, provided the additional help. Elliott became increasingly reliant on his parents' help, which they provided too quickly, thereby not giving Elliott sufficient experience to work on his own.

How could Elliott's parents help him gain confidence and become more independent in his homework habits? By being involved in Elliott's school work, his parents were off to a good start. They taught him, by example, that homework is important and needs to be taken seriously. With time they can help him become more independent in his work habits by providing reinforcement and support. Repetition through practice, patience, and success are critical for some children to develop the self-confidence and habits necessary to complete homework successfully. As Elliott's confidence improves, his parents could gradually *reduce* their support and encourage Elliott to work more independently.

How involved should you be? That depends on how much your child needs your assistance. Asking about homework and helping out is an important part of your guiding role as a parent, especially for elementary-aged children who are having difficulty learning independent homework skills. You should try to establish a working relationship with your child, a homework alliance, in which you have an agreed upon time, place, and system for completing and monitoring homework each day. On the other hand, parents who are too involved in their child's homework may stifle their child's ability to do homework independently. Parents should be available for assistance and feedback. They should not actually correct their child's homework or do it for them.

When Your Child Repeatedly Makes Excuses to Avoid Doing Homework

Children often think of many reasons why they didn't complete their homework.
"It was too hard!"
"I didn't understand it."
"I forgot to copy it down."
"I left my books in school."
"My teacher didn't explain it."
"I didn't have time."

The involved parent is familiar enough with their child's ability and homework habits to know when they are really struggling with homework or when they are using excuses to avoid homework. Children who make excuses for not completing homework, even though they have the understanding, the skill, and the opportunity to complete it successfully, must be held responsible for their behavior. When confronted they may get into lengthy discussions to defend their actions. Such discussions often result in fruitless debates. In this situation, a specific plan to solve the homework problem is necessary. Follow these steps:

- Encourage your child to take responsibility for homework, and don't allow yourself to get trapped in lengthy discussions or arguments. The message to your child should be clear: Homework (or a percentage of it) must be completed.

- Set up "homework rules" that you and your child can agree to follow. These rules provide structure and should include such things as when, where, and how homework should be done. Post these "homework rules" in your child's room and refer to them when a problem arises. Children will see them as rule-based decisions, rather than arbitrary commands.

- Help your child make short-term homework goals that can gradually be extended. Some children become overwhelmed by the thought of too much homework. They need your help to break assignments down into "bite-sized chunks," which may be easier for them to manage. Each time a "chunk" is finished, offer some break time and encourage the child to tackle the next part of the assignment.

- Reinforce and praise appropriate homework behavior and avoid getting into a negative pattern of scolding, nagging, or threatening your child. This will only increase frustration and tension, usually worsening the problem.

When Your Child
Doesn't Understand Homework

It is common for children to become frustrated when they do not have a clear understanding of the material presented in class or when homework is too difficult for them to master on their own. Only 7 percent of high school students explained they purposely chose not to complete their homework.[1] Confusion about an assignment is a common reason for incomplete homework. When children are confused about homework, they can either ask for help, struggle with it on their own and eventually find a solution, give up, or avoid the assignment altogether. Confusion is more likely to occur for all children during a new task or when a new concept has been presented at school.

If a child is dawdling over homework, one of the first things a parent should do is check to see if the child understands the assignment. Sometimes we assume the child is being resistant when, in fact, the child may be embarrassed to admit to being confused and ask for help.

Difficulty understanding homework is a common problem for children with learning disabilities, especially in the area of their specific learning disability (e.g., math, reading). Parents of children with learning difficulties may have an even greater challenge in knowing how to effectively help their children. Many of these children will require more practice before something is learned. Their parents need to be very patient and supportive. However, children with learning disabilities often report that their parents get angry when helping them with such subjects as reading and spelling.[2]

Difficulties understanding and following directions are frequent problems for students with poor organizational skills (e.g., students with attentional problems). These students fail to attend to important information, either in class or in written instructions. This is especially true if the information is lengthy, embedded in several words, or presented in a complex visual array.

Investigate whether your child's problem is the result of confusion over what to do or how to do it. If you find that the problem is a result of your child's confusion, or that it reflects poor ability, it is essential that you and your child's teacher develop a system to communicate clearly and consistently about homework assignments. Some ways to accomplish this are explained below.

Communication Tips

✎ Set up a system of color coded homework folders (e.g., work going home goes in a green folder, work coming back in a red folder). This will help your child remain organized.

✎ If your child must write down homework assignments independently, have your child use a colored pencil so the notations can be quickly located and reviewed by your child's teacher before your child leaves school each day.

✎ Ask the teacher to assign a homework buddy. At the end of a period or a day, your child and a buddy can make certain that they each understand the assignment and what must be done that evening. If there is disagreement, they can seek clarification from the teacher.

✎ If understanding written assignments is a problem for your child, try other forms of communication (e.g., visual or auditory). For instance, reduce the information by using highlighters to underline the important parts. Other good home helpers are to ask your child to read directions aloud, rewrite them, or explain them to you before beginning.

✎ Consider the possibility that your child's difficulty understanding directions for homework may be part of a larger problem related to a specific language deficit, learning disability, attention or auditory processing disorder. Discuss this possibility with teachers and consider referral for screening to a school or community-based professional.

✎ Consider that the same problems that cause your child to have difficulty understanding homework instructions may also impair your child's ability to follow directions in other situations in class (e.g., taking tests). Your child may need direct instruction to learn effective test taking skills or listening strategies.

When Your Child Waits Until the Last Minute to Start Homework Assignments

Everyone procrastinates to some extent. Avoiding an unpleasant task in exchange for doing something more pleasurable is common in children and adults. Some children get stuck in a "procrastination holding pattern," which can seriously affect performance in school. They don't get started on daily homework assignments until late in the day or evening, put off working on long-term projects, and fail to study for tests in advance. Procrastination may simply be a form of initial resistance to a less than pleasant task. In severe cases, procrastination can lead to serious academic problems.

You can help your child get out of the procrastination habit by following the suggestions below.

- With the help of your child, choose a pleasant place for completing homework.

- Create an agreed upon schedule and routine for homework in that place of study.

- Have your child make a checklist of the tasks that need to be done. This can include ranking the assignments in any way the child chooses (e.g., from easy to hard).

- Once the setting, the schedule, and the task order are established, provide appropriate supervision.

- To create an incentive, you can restrict a number of pleasurable activities until some or all homework is completed.

- Your child may want to create a sense of urgency. One way to do this is by using a timer or setting goals to accomplish work in a specific period to have access to the preferred activity.

When Your Child Takes Too Long to Complete Homework

Many children start their homework without difficulty, but find it difficult to stay on task long enough to complete it. In these households, parents spend a great deal of time getting their child to refocus attention to homework. In severe cases, it can take many more hours than it should to complete homework. Needless to say, this can be extremely frustrating for both the parent and the child. Parents and children often become irritable and lose their temper. Homework sessions become battlegrounds—a tug of war between the parent who wants homework completed and the child who tries to avoid doing it at all costs.

Children may have trouble staying on-task to complete homework for a number of reasons. Some children simply have trouble sustaining attention to tasks, particularly when the task is repetitive and requires attention to details. A child with ADHD has difficulty paying attention for any length of time. (We will discuss ADHD later.) For other children, inattention may be the result of confusion about the assignment. These children may not understand the instructions or the procedure to be used in completing their homework assignment; they lose interest and move off-task. Other children find homework boring and appear disinterested in learning and achieving a satisfactory grade.

Parents typically react to this kind of problem by keeping a close watch over their child during homework time. They help the child get started and supervise work closely. Whenever the child goes off task, the parent reminds the child to get back to work. The child may take the prompt (some call it "nagging") and starts back to work for a short time until the next prompt. Both the parent and the child interact this way nightly.

Let's examine why this type of interaction is usually unproductive. When parents prompt (or nag) about homework, most children temporarily go on-task to stop the prompting. As long as they are on-task, parents usually stop prompting. As long as parents prompt, homework gets done. Children do their work for the wrong reason; they try to eliminate the pressure put on them. Each time parents engage in this process the likelihood is increased that the process will be repeated. Unfortunately, children are not learning independent homework skills, and parents are placed in the position of becoming homework guards.

The first step you should take to end this cycle is to focus your attention on the positive aspects of your child's behavior rather than the negative. Try the suggestions below.

Focusing on the Positive Builds Success

✎ Reinforce your child with praise and rewards while your child is engaging in appropriate homework behavior, even if it is for a short period of time.

✎ Encourage your child to work for longer periods independently by establishing work-time goals or work-production goals. A work-time goal might be a specific number of minutes of on-task behavior that earns a reward when achieved. A work-production goal might be a specific number of examples completed (pages read, questions answered,

etc.) that earns a reward when achieved. Gradually extend the work-time or work-production goals to increase your child's length of independent work. Continue to provide consistent, frequent positive reinforcement.

✎ Avoid falling into the nagging trap when your child is off-task; provide a positive incentive instead. It is helpful to offer rewards and incentives to your child for appropriate homework behavior.

✎ Withhold preferred activities (e.g., television time) until homework goals are accomplished.

When Your Child Rushes Through Homework and Makes Careless Errors

Some children rush through their homework but do it thoroughly and correctly. In general, this is not a problem. However, others rush to complete homework and make numerous careless errors, hand in sloppy work, or fail to pay attention to the directions. These children need to work at a slower pace and check their assignments for accuracy.

If your child sacrifices homework accuracy for speed, try following these suggestions:

✎ Review homework assignments nightly, checking for thoroughness, neatness, and accuracy. Encourage your child to correct any mistakes.

✎ Have your child underline or highlight important words or phrases in the "directions" portion of an assignment to make certain the directions were read.

✎ Emphasize that you want your child to do their "best work" on homework, not their "fastest work."

✎ Train your child to self-monitor homework production by checking for errors in spelling, punctuation, neatness, calculations, correct heading, etc. Provide additional "bonus" privileges (e.g., extra TV time, etc.) if you find they have completed work neatly and accurately.

✎ Withhold privileges (e.g., TV time, phone time, etc.) until you are satisfied your child has put forth the best effort possible and has completed homework accurately. However, if you suspect errors in homework are due to poor understanding rather than hasty completion, provide assistance as needed.

✎ Some children have handwriting difficulty caused by visual motor problems. This may make it very hard for them to write neatly. Asking them to redo homework to be neater is often fruitless. If this is the case for your child, overlook neatness and pay attention more to accuracy and thoroughness. For some assignments, creative ideas and interesting plots are more important initially than grammar or handwriting. Make sure you understand the lesson objective.

When Your Child Lacks Confidence to Do Homework Independently

The opinions children develop about themselves and their ability to succeed in school are very important. Parents sometimes put unreasonable pressure on their child to perform at too high a level. In some homes, the process of completing homework drains parents and children emotionally. Although the work is completed, children in these situations often do not feel good about themselves, their abilities, or their work.

It is often difficult for parents to recognize the process by which children develop helpless feelings about school and homework. Due to learning problems or behavioral disabilities, a child may experience many small academic failures at school in comparison to his or her classmates. Hearing a constant stream of negative comments can affect a child's academic self esteem, especially when that child makes comparisons with siblings or peers who receive fewer negative comments. Negative feedback decreases students' interest or willingness to engage in homework.

Children struggling at school often perceive themselves as ineffective students. They see themselves as destined to fail, and they see others as having all the answers. Even when they have opportunities to succeed, they make only minimal efforts because they believe their actions will not alter the outcome. They may engage in whatever activities necessary to avoid homework by quitting, avoiding, cheating, clowning, becoming passive, denying, rushing, or complaining.

Try some of these solutions:

✎ Listen carefully to your child. If you perceive that your child's self-confidence is low with respect to school performance, it will be important to structure homework and other school related activities to increase success. Try to place your child on a diet of successful experiences and praise. Keep the focus positive.

✎ Emphasize your child's strengths rather than his or her weaknesses.

✎ When you review homework, start with what has been completed correctly before focusing on revisions.

✎ If your child is receiving more homework than can be handled in one night, speak to the teacher(s) and explain the problem. Teachers are often willing to make adjustments in quantity of homework assigned when they understand a problem exists.

When Your Child Complains that Homework Is Boring

If children understand what to do and how to do it, moving off task may indicate they have grown tired of sitting or working on that task and are experiencing difficulty sustaining interest or effort. This is a common problem with homework assignments for all children. Failure on your part to understand this phenomenon can result in you becoming angry over an issue with which we all struggle—boredom due to repetition. Boredom is even more likely to occur during a practice or review task, particularly late in the day or in the evening when children are tired. If sustaining attention or ADHD is a problem, your child will seek to replace a repetitive, boring task with a more interesting activity or a daydream.

It is important for you to help your child create a balance between work and enjoyment. Help

your child become part of the solution rather than the problem. Ask your child for ideas on what might help and try them out.

If you perceive the work to be lengthy, repetitive, and effortful, acknowledge it. Consider offering an increasingly attractive reward for work completion. For many children you will need to take smaller steps. That is, after you have broken the assignment into parts with checkpoints, offer rewards as each part is completed. These rewards might be as simple as five minute breaks or allowing the child to alternate between several tasks (e.g., spelling and reading). Children differ with respect to how long they can work on a task before getting bored or restless. This depends on the type of task the child is performing. Once children reach their limit, it is time for a break, a preferred activity, a snack, or a change of task.

As a broader solution, consider communicating with your child's teacher concerning a modification of homework assignments:

✎ offering more choices of topics, methods of reporting, etc;

✎ emphasizing demonstration of concepts and problem solving rather than memorizing assignments; or

✎ reducing length of assignments (e.g., completing five math problems to demonstrate mastery rather than 20, several smaller assignments or chapters rather than one long assignment or report).

When Your Child Has a Learning Disability

Some children struggling with school work in class or at home suffer from an undiagnosed learning disability. Difficulty completing homework has been documented for more than half of students with learning disabilities.[3] Due to learning disabilities, many children react to homework by daydreaming, procrastinating, and have difficulty working independently. These behaviors may represent the coping strategies some children use when they do not understand what to do or lack the confidence to work alone. A large percentage of teachers reported that they did not routinely discuss or review assignments with their students with learning disabilities. They also did not give feedback on homework or incorporate homework into grading.[4] This indicates that teachers, like parents, may fall into the trap of assuming that these students know what to do and how to do it, when this is probably not the case.

Parents aware of the signs exhibited by children with learning disabilities are in position to seek appropriate help for their child from a school or community-based professional. Specific learning disability is defined as achievement that is lower in one or more academic areas than would be predicted from IQ potential. There are two types of learning disabilities—a larger number of students have deficits in verbal learning. These skills are required for talking, reading, and composition. There are also many students with visual learning disabilities which leads to problems in math or social learning. In both verbal and nonverbal types of learning disabilities deficits tend to be in the basic skill areas. However, failure to develop basic skills delays the development of comprehension and problem solving, which are advanced types of skills. Children with the problems discussed below continue to struggle to achieve academically.

Problems in Reading, Spelling, and Writing.

The ability to identify words or decode is an essential school skill. Just to recognize words, children must learn to follow print across the page from left to right and to translate written symbols to sounds, which become words. In this process they must recognize that a written symbol, such as a "b" represents a sound that is different from a "d."

A child who cannot grasp the basic skill of decoding will not be able to read or spell in meaningful or pleasurable ways. Once children learn to read, their energies can be directed toward understanding the meaning of the reading material (encoding). Learning to decode and encode words requires concentration, energy, coordination, and the integration of many skills.

It is probable that children with reading difficulties will have trouble with spelling. However, some children who read well still have difficulties remembering how to spell. The reason for this is that the process of recognizing words (reading decoding) is much easier than the process of recalling the sounds and images of words (spelling). Spelling requires that children recall those images as needed when asked to write words or stories. Thus, the basic skill of spelling is fundamental for writing. If children struggle with spelling, they will find it difficult to progress in writing, and written assignments are often an integral part of children's homework.

Finally, handwriting is considered a basic skill. Students who have poor visual-motor skill (e.g., children with ADHD) will be slower, work harder, and tire more easily when asked to do a handwriting task.[5] Research by the first author at Purdue University revealed that gifted elementary level children also may have difficulty with handwriting tasks, probably because their ideas come much faster than they can express them in writing.

If your child is struggling to develop the basic skills necessary to decode, spell, or write, homework will be a laborious, time consuming, and often frustrating experience. If this is a problem for your child, accommodations must be made for homework, because your child will have the additional work to "catch up" on basic skills as well as the current requirements of the assigned classwork. Unfortunately, since your child is experiencing trouble catching up, keeping up will be an additional responsibility. This unrealistic expectation is often placed upon your shoulders.

Learning to read and spell are a bit like learning to play the piano. First you must practice scales to play more fluently. But along the way, good piano teachers also provide students with plenty of opportunities to play actual music. Students will lose interest in playing if only required to practice the scales. Reading instruction works the same way. To become a reader, a child must not only master words but also view books as a source of pleasure and information. It is therefore important that you help your child keep a balance, if they are struggling with reading. You can do this by providing your child with high interest-low ability books or by reading to your child.

Consider also that if your child experiences reading problems, you might acquaint yourself with the school's reading curriculum. Some teachers use one method to teach reading (e.g., a sight memory approach, a phonics approach). When teachers use only one method, children who might learn better by a different method may have greater difficulty. Teachers who use a variety of approaches to teach reading often have fewer children with reading problems.

Of course, children working hard to decode or recognize words will have difficulty remembering and understanding what they read (reading encoding). But other children learn to read (decode) quickly and still have difficulty understanding what they read. These children may sound like expert readers but be unable to tell you what happened in a story they just read. They may begin to struggle when attempting to learn from reading at about the third grade.

Similarly, children may have learned to spell but the curriculum expects them to move from forming simple words to expressing their ideas in writing. If your child is having difficulty with either comprehending what is read or using words to convey meaning in written assignments, remediation needs to begin with understanding spoken language. Finally, they may have plenty of story ideas and good writing skills, but have few strategies about how to organize those ideas. Remediation here needs to begin with organizing spoken language.

If you are not sure whether your child's problems are with reading decoding or reading comprehension, pay attention to your child's spoken language skills. If your child speaks easily and coherently, is able to listen well, understands and can explain what is being said, then your child's problem understanding reading probably lies in the reading decoding process. In contrast, if a child has difficulty with readng comprehension or verbal expression, the problem may be in the language comprehension and self-expression process.

Problems with Basic Math Processes and Problem Solving.

Similar to learning to recognize and spell words, performing computations involves the skills of memorizing facts and sequences of steps, visualizing, and fine motor control, as well as initial learning about the correspondence between quantities and number symbols.

Many children struggle with math homework because they have not achieved an understanding of basic concepts or mastered the underlying pre-requisite skills. If your child had problems developing counting or the concept of one-to-one correspondence, it is likely that learning basic mathematics skills will be difficult. If you recognize that your child simply does not understand math assignments, this is likely the problem. It will be essential for you to develop an understanding of your child's math weaknesses, advocate with teachers, and seek additional help or support, if necessary.

If your child experiences computational problems, there are a number of simpler strategies that are effective. Math computation, especially in the speed of calculating computations, is an area in which students with ADHD are more likely to fall behind their classmates.[6] Their slow speed may be due to a failure to sustain attention to repetition and thus to overlearn rote skills. These problems may be remediated when teachers use concrete objects whereby children have direct experience with manipulating items in combination with manipulating mathematical symbols.

Some children learn basic computational processes but have trouble with math problem solving. This is similar to those children who learn to decode but then have trouble with reading comprehension. Language weaknesses or difficulty with reading mathematics problems may make it difficult for them to understand math presented by the teacher verbally or by written instruction. Another type of problem is thinking with visual images, which may make it difficult to picture problems, think in three dimensions, or interpret charts and graphs. If your child learned math facts easily but by fourth grade began to struggle, your child may be experiencing a specific problem related to the ability to think with more abstract visual information (i.e., understanding, estimating, or representing size, distance, time, space, quantities). For example, Michael, a fifth grader with weaknesses in the skills required for understanding complex language and thinking, does not understand where to begin when reading a math story problem. When the teacher showed him a picture of four trees and asked how many one-half of them would be he responded, "You mean if I cut them this way?" Then he made the motions of drawing a horizontal line through the middle of the four trees. Clearly, Michael will require help interpreting language

and learning to use strategies to problem solve before being asked to complete such problems.

If you are going to assist your child with completing math homework, it is important for you to understand the curriculum and how your child is being taught. Most schools offer a balanced curriculum that emphasizes the understanding and use of math concepts in applied situations rather than focusing on teaching simple, memorized computational skills.

When Your Child Has ADHD

Many parents and teachers assume that when children do not pay attention to their schoolwork it is because they choose not to pay attention. Parents and teachers often focus on the problem being one of choice rather than ability. They view inattention as noncompliance rather than a disability.

Students with ADHD are often the types of students about whom parents and teachers make these assumptions. From research conducted at Purdue University, we have identified several characteristics that separate students with ADHD from their classmates. Among these characteristics are a dislike of homework and a dislike of long-term projects which often require work at home. Even gifted students with ADHD were described by their teachers as either not doing homework or as working hard at school to avoid taking it home. "He absolutely hates homework so he works very hard at not having homework," stated one teacher about a gifted student with ADHD.

Unfortunately, students with ADHD face a risk of school failure two to three times greater than that of other children without disabilities and with equivalent intelligence.[7] Students with ADHD have difficulty sticking to most homework assignments. This is likely due to the fact that homework typically is repetitive, effortful, uninteresting, offers little immediate gratification, and is done with little one-on-one supervision. When students with ADHD cannot sustain attention or maintain interest in a task any longer, they look elsewhere. They attempt to create stimulation for themselves by moving around, by daydreaming, or focusing outward to changes in their environment.

Why Children with ADHD Have Difficulty Completing Homework

Poor sustained attention translates into difficulty sticking to repetitive, relatively uninteresting activities that require effort and are not of the child's choosing. This defines most homework assignments. An attentional preference for external stimulation also makes it difficult for these children to selectively attend to their own internal thoughts, plans, goals, and homework strategies. Finally, children with ADHD have a strong need to act and to minimize the amount of time they have to wait for gratification.

Thus, children with ADHD are frequently repeat offenders, and their finished products typically under-represent their abilities. This leads to frustration on your part and increased conflict when you pressure your child to complete work more carefully That is, these students require more supervision, yet when supervision is provided, they often become increasingly resistant, oppositional, or overly dependent.

The solution to the homework problem for children with ADHD appears to lie in our ability to make homework interesting, to make payoffs valuable, to assign homework that focuses on process (e.g., problem solving, observing, and recording) rather than repetition (e.g., 50 math problems of the same type), and for parents to intersperse homework periods with enjoyable activities. The more interesting a task or the more attractive a pay-off, the more likely the child with

ADHD will engage in homework.

Usually parents use coercive or negative consequences when they assume their child is willfully not paying attention to homework assignments. In the case of a child with ADHD, the parent may be pushing their child for something the child cannot control or can only control for a short time. In this case, punishment does not lead to better attention. It leads to greater anger and frustration for parents and children.

We have developed several positive ways to address the homework problems of children with ADHD. Based on our research at Purdue University, we have found that these students need, prefer, and perform better with novel and active tasks than do their peers. Students with ADHD are attentive to something at all moments, but their attentional focus is pulled toward what most interests them. Interest is defined generally by what is colorful, intense, moving, changing, unusual, unexpected, or personally meaningful. We can guide children's attention by using what captivates them or by using some of the following suggestions:

- ✎ Provide colored magic markers for underlining directions to guide a child's attention to important information.

- ✎ Encourage the child's teacher to allow the child to cross out the incorrect answers (rather than correct answers) on multiple choice tests to prevent impulsive responses.

- ✎ Allow the child to have some choice in where, when, and in what order to do homework—provided their choices seem reasonable.

- ✎ Alter homework assignments so they can be completed with structured motor responses (e.g., turning flash cards, sorting things). Action can reinforce attention in children with ADHD.

✎   Use games and challenging physical activities for practice tasks but not for tasks that have not been practiced.

✎   Students with ADHD are likely to ignore important information that is neutral, ambiguous, subtle, small, or detailed. Add color to important information during new or complex homework tasks to make it more attractive to the child. Some parents may find it useful to use a "Reading Ruler" (available from the A.D.D. WareHouse 800-233-9273), which provides a yellow see-through window that the child can use to track lines of print.

✎   At the end of a task or when boredom and fatigue set in, increase the novelty of the task or shorten the assignment, if necessary.

✎   Provide activity breaks that the child can look forward to after completing a certain quantity of work.

When Your Child
is Struggling with
Emotions, Behavior, or Development

When it comes to your child's emotions, behavior, and development, trust your judgment. Seek professional help and set up a long term plan if you believe your child is struggling.

If your child is under 10 years of age and experiences significant difficulty with conduct—displaying serious aggressiveness, bullying or intimidating peers, being deliberately cruel to animals, stealing or lying repeatedly, setting fires, habitually and seriously violating rules, being truant from school, running away, or even staying out all night—seek professional help.

It is often easier to make the decision to seek help when your child experiences problems that disrupt you and others. It is often more difficult to know when to seek help if your child is experiencing problems related to emotional distress—anxiety or depression.

Anxious children often worry so much about the quality and adequacy of their homework that they become perfectionists. They begin avoiding or continually redo homework to avoid failure.

Depressed children often appear gloomy, sad, and angry. They often experience strong feelings of helplessness and hopelessness, which not only disturbs their daily activities but leads to chronic homework problems. Depressed children often have minor physical ailments such as stomachaches or headaches without clear cause. They may experience changes in their patterns of sleep, appetite, energy, or overall health. Their sadness often interferes with concentration. They may be moody, angry, and socially isolated. If you have noticed a change in your child's moods or emotions or a recent decline in their school work combined with social isolation and apparent sadness and anger, professional consultation is advisable.

Family physicians, pediatricians, and school psychologists or counselors are often good first contacts. However, we believe the letters after the professionals name—M.D., Ph.D., or LCSW—are only as important as the professional's dedication and willingness to take the time necessary to understand your concerns.

Summary

In this step we have identified and discussed 11 problems children commonly have with completing homework. Children who exhibit these problems may not have acquired the seven essential homework skills discussed in step two. Sometimes parents and children develop patterns acting and reacting with one another that are unproductive and contribute to these problems as well.

You have read through the common problems parents experience when managing their child's homework and you have some idea of what solutions to try. Don't stop reading this workbook, there is more important information to follow.

Read on! You are now ready for step five—Building the Learning Station.™

STEP 5
Building the Learning Station™

Step 5
Building the Learning Station™

In previous steps we have identified seven skills children need to learn and practice to manage homework independently. We have also identified many things parents can do at home, which will have a positive effect on children's work in school and homework. In this step, we will show you how to build the Learning Station™. We will explain why it could become a very important tool in helping your child learn the skills necessary to complete homework independently.

The Learning Station™ is a relatively simple device that will help your child complete more homework with greater accuracy and in less time! The Learning Station™ is based on research that has demonstrated improved performance and persistence. The Learning Station™ is a free standing, three sided, pegboard panel. Children place it on a desk in front of them as they complete work. The Learning Station™ is portable and can be placed in any room of the house or in a classroom.

The Learning Station™ is not an isolation booth. It may appear that the Learning Station™ blocks the child's view and therefore reduces distractions. However, this is not the purpose of the Learning Station.™ Other devices designed specifically to reduce such distractions (e.g., study carrels) have not been found to improve performance.[1] In contrast, the Learning Station™ has been developed as a system to help your child organize homework tasks, work, maintain interest, and improve self-management.

A Workplace to Develop Organizational Skills

The Learning Station™ is designed to help your child become more organized and develop efficient work habits. Efficient work habits allow your child to complete assignments within a reasonable time schedule and produce work as quickly as his/her abilities will allow.

The Learning Station™ contains places in each of the three panels to hold supplies and related materials. Work to be completed is placed in a folder in the left panel and moved to a folder in the right panel when finished. The Learning Station™ also helps your child practice how to break up homework time into work and break activities. After a certain amount of work is completed, the Learning Station™ is also a place where reinforcement activities are available.

A Workplace to Maintain Interest

The Learning Station™ addresses your child's need for fun, especially during the performance of familiar tasks. All of us require stimulation or change if we are to maintain maximum performance.[2] Children achieve such stimulation by moving or using their senses (sight, hearing, taste, touch, smell). They are more likely to seek stimulation by talking, moving, responding impulsively or intensely, and looking around at changes in their environments (inattention) during the performance of familiar, long, or difficult tasks. This "sensation-seeking" behavior occurs particularly in settings that do not allow activity or that require waiting with nothing to do.

These characteristics are true for all children, especially at younger ages. However, they occur earlier, more often, and with greater intensity for students with impulse or attention problems, as well as those diagnosed with ADHD. These children appear to lose interest faster. At Purdue University over the last two decades, we have found that students with ADHD can look and perform more like average learners when they are provided with stimulation (e.g., color, opportunities for activity) in their environments.

Based on these research findings, we have designed a stimulation component to the Learning Station™. Its purpose is to make the learning environment fun and help your child sustain attention to assignments. The following types of stimulation are built into the Learning Station™.

Color. The Learning Station™ will be decorated by you and your child in bright colors. There will be places to attach supplies, work to be done, and completed work. These too will be color coded.

Physical activity. For all children, moving and talking improves their ability to pay attention. For this reason, the routine used with the Learning Station™ breaks homework up with five minute breaks for brief activities of interest.

Choice. The opportunities for choice are provided by allowing your child (a) to decide where s/he will use the Learning Station™ and (b) to identify five to seven brief five minute activities s/he can use during breaks. You will need to devote some time to these two activities. Students in our study created some activities for themselves.[3] Alan chose to draw, shoot baskets, eat, stretch, play with his dog, and clean his room. Anita chose to eat a snack, chat with Mom, play with her cat, clean her room, run around the block, get clothes out for the next day, and draw. Shane chose to watch television, eat a snack, chat with his Mom, run, and work on a model. Notice that for two of the children, cleaning their room or parts of their room was seen as a more rewarding activity than was homework. This makes sense when you see that cleaning a room is active and involves a change from a sedentary homework task.

Music. While working, your child could listen to music of his/her choice. Remember how we reported that music helps all children pay attention? It is especially helpful for older students and those with attentional problems. If the music is familiar children will not be distracted by the words. If the music is not familiar, it will be best used during a practice type of task and not during an assignment that requires careful thinking (e.g., writing a report).

You may want to work with your child to create tapes with a music work-interval and brief periods (e.g., five minutes) of break-intervals with no music. The music stops during the five minute breaks and starts again during the work interval. If you cannot make these tapes together, you may want to simply use the kitchen timer—turn off the music at the end of the work interval and reset the timer for the amount of time for the break interval. In either case you will need to accumulate tapes or CDs with your child.

A Workplace to Increase Independence

To work independently and successfully, children need to focus their own thoughts and be efficient at retrieving previously learned strategies and appropriate behavior. For many children, paying attention to these internal aspects of the self must be learned. In particular, students with ADHD have strong preferences for external stimulation (i.e., what they can see, hear, smell, and touch). When attention is directed outwards, attention to the self is decreased.[4] For example, if you are paying attention to something moving in your external environment, you will focus less on your internal physical state and be less aware of that state (e.g., feel less pain). Parents often use this distraction or redirection technique to move their children's minds off of pain, hunger, or frustration.

In using the Learning Station™, your goal is to help your child develop a balance between internal and external focus. To be an efficient, independent worker, your child needs to remember and use previously learned internalized homework strategies. These are strategies the child can access by focusing attention inwardly. Your child must also evaluate his or her ongoing performance (external) to make sure that the work being produced is meeting known standards (internal) of accuracy and neatness.

A simple strategy, the use of a mirror, has been found to increase self-awareness and thereby improve accuracy and persistence on simple tasks. In a series of research studies at Purdue University, independent work increased dramatically when a mirror was present. In a recent study, the mirror was placed into the Learning Station™ and math completion and accuracy of homework was evaluated. The Learning Station™ with the mirror produced an increase in math homework completion and accuracy that was three times what it had been before the Learning Station™ was introduced.

The Learning Station™ will also help your child develop a self-monitoring system. This involves having your child enter information on a log sheet at certain time periods. For example, your child will enter the number of problems that were completed during the work interval of time before beginning the preferred activity break interval. The log sheet will also have an optional place for you to sign when homework is completed.

Building the Learning Station™

The Learning Station™ is a free standing, three sided, pegboard panel. Pegboard is sold in local hardware or lumber stores. Ask the store to cut three 16 inch square panels. The panels can be connected with small screws into hinges, two to a side, placed an equal distance from each other. If you are not mechanically inclined, the panels can be attached using strips of duct tape on front and back. Lay the three panels down on a flat surface, tape one side extending the edges of the tape over and folding them back on the next side. Turn over and repeat the process. Although not as effective as hinges, duct tape will work. The board can be spray painted with a bright color of your child's choice.

When you purchase the pegboard, also purchase a package of pegboard clips. These clips will fit into the pegboard allowing you to hang the materials to be contained on the board. The left panel will contain a folder for log sheets and a smaller folder for activity cards. Each folder should be a different color and can be hung from the pegboard by hole punching the colored folders and hanging them on the clips. The log sheets (see next page) are made up of three columns that are labeled "Work Completed" and "Break." The sheet also contains a place for your child's name, a place for the date, day, beginning and ending times, and a place for your signature. The folder containing the log sheets can be as simple as half of a trapper holder as pictured below. Also on the left side is a smaller folder containing activity cards.

A 12 inch or close, square mirror should be hung on the middle panel. Finally, the right panel contains a different color folder for completed log sheets, pencil holder, and a small cassette player.

The Learning Station™

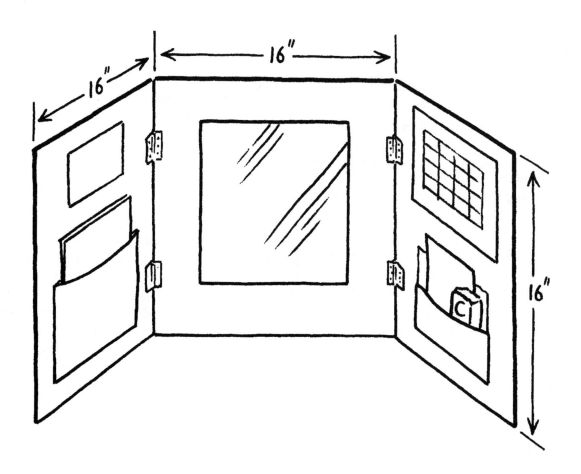

LOG SHEET

Child's Name _____   Date _____

Beginning Time _____   Ending Time _____

Parent's Signature _____

Work Completed	(Break)	Work Completed	(Break)	Work Completed	(Break)
Example: math problems # 1-7	(play with dog)	spelling -write sent.	(15 min. TV)	math problems 8-20	(snack)

Instructions to Your Child

Once the Learning Station™ is built, each aspect should be explained to your child. Your child should be provided with the following list of steps as the Learning Station™ is introduced.

1. Enter the date, day, and beginning time on the Log Sheet.
2. Take out necessary materials.
3. Start the music tape and begin working.
4. When the work interval time is over and the music stops, make a note on the Log Sheet of what you have completed during the past prearranged time (e.g., 15 minutes).
5. Choose an activity break from the choice pocket and do it for the length of the break-interval (e.g., five minutes) until the music comes back on.
6. Return to work and repeat the previous two steps until your homework is completed.
7. When you have finished, log the time and have one of your parents sign the log.

Troubleshooting

Problem

Your child experiences difficulty completing longer assignments at the Learning Station™.

Solution

It is important for you to help your child learn how to divide tasks into parts, sequence those parts, and provide sufficient time for those parts to be completed. How can you teach this in a fun way?

Sometimes we use a peanut butter and jelly sandwich to teach children about task analysis. First, ask your child to tell you how to make a peanut butter and jelly sandwich so that another child could make one by reading your child's recipe. Take notes on everything your child says. Second, put each step on a separate piece of paper or index card. Then, ask your child to make sure the order is correct and whether there needs to be any additions or changes. Next, try to make the sandwich following each step exactly as it is written. Finally, when you get stuck, ask your child whether he/she needs to reorder the cards or add cards until all the steps in the sequence are correct.

Once your child can analyze this task, take your child to another enjoyable activity, such as planning to have a friend overnight. What would all the steps be to get permission and set up activities for having a friend spend the night? When your child is successful with breaking plans into parts, you can then add possible times when each step will be completed.

Using index cards to make the planning visual, concrete, and easy to re-order is an excellent way of developing this process. There are other ways to plan steps and deadlines. For example, you might begin with a time line drawn horizontally across a piece of paper and ask your child to suggest which dates should be included below the line. When your child sees the times written out, he/she can add steps to be completed and pin those events to the time-line. For younger children, you might use a clothes line and put index cards on the line. Once your child understands this process, you can begin breaking down homework assignments using similar procedures.

Problem

Difficulty remaining on task, even when using the Learning Station™. Although most children can work for a period of time on a task they understand, all children tire of a task after working beyond their limits.

Solution

Children differ in how long they can work on a task before becoming bored or restless. How long can your child work before he or she begins to lose concentration? If you know approximately how long your child will sit and work independently, you can expect that length of time for studying. Once your child has reached his or her limit, which partially depends on the type of task your child is performing, it is time for a break, a preferred activity, a snack or a change of task. This type of system is incorporated into the Learning Station™.

Children work better with concentrated effort if they are motivated to reach a goal. If the preferred activity break is working well, but your child has become bored with the activity, it may be time to select new activities. Maybe some breaks need to be silly things. Some children will even work hard on their assignments if they have five minutes to daydream.

One of the children in our research study told us that he became tired of listening to the same music.[5] We suggest that you let children select their own music for the work interval. You can use a kitchen timer that your child can set for each work interval. Your child could also set the timer for the break interval. Although we suggest a five-minute break, you may need to begin with longer break intervals or shorter work intervals. The five-minute break interval worked very well for our students in middle school, but it might need to be adapted for younger children.

In addition to breaks and planned change, you can help your child by making tasks more fun. For example, some parents have made a large hopscotch game, which is used to practice multiplication. Their children jump the number sequence and land on the answers! One way to make tasks more fun is to select topic areas of interest to your child. Interesting topics are especially important for tasks that require your child to think or plan a response (e.g., composing stories or generating solutions to problems). However, even with high interest topics, thinking ahead is still difficult due to the requirements for delaying activity while thinking. Give your child something to do to help your child handle the delay while thinking or listening to others speak. For example, during the performance of these tasks you can give your child big, colored, fuzzy pipe cleaners, small sponges, or coated wire to manipulate. These "work toys" can be kept in additional pockets in the Learning Station™.

Problem

Some children find it very difficult to assess their progress. They feel distressed because they worry about future assignments without focusing on their accomplishments.

Solution

In addition to the mirror, we suggest you use methods to help your child pay attention and be aware of internal thoughts, feelings, standards, and strategies. For example, asking your child questions about his or her perceptions, opinions, and feelings directs attention inward. Using diaries or encouraging your child's use of fantasy/make believe also require a reflective, inward look. With respect to the Learning Station™, we suggest that you video tape your child doing homework and ask your child to review it later. Your child can comment on what he/she was thinking or doing at various times during the tape. Tapes can be made of various subject areas and in different rooms of the house for later analysis.

We also suggest that you consider helping your child develop different methods of self-monitoring. Self-monitoring is particularly difficult for children with ADHD. They struggle to plan and reflect on their actions (self-checking). All children appear to work optimally in the presence of immediate cues. To help them plan the future and evaluate past performances, we need to help them make plans visually and check their work in interesting ways. Both of these types of past and future performances require children to take the role of coach or director rather than the role of immediate actor. The roles of coach and director need to be encouraged in these children.

To plan ahead, children must be able to select goals. If children set their own goals, they will be more likely to focus on those goals. This is true even if your child has not written down the steps that are needed to achieve these goals. It will be necessary, however, for your child to periodically review these goals and make certain that they have not already been attained.

Goals can be written in different areas. Some might be related to homework. But others might be related to friends or projects. You might suggest goals for your child, if your child does not know where to begin. It is important, however, for your child to select goals that are meaningful. If you find that your child is not working toward a goal, it should be revised and made more meaningful to your child.

Once your child has selected several goals, your child is now ready to create a plan for moving in that direction. This is an optional step. A step that your child must agree is worthwhile. If your child has progressed this far, you are doing amazingly well! Perhaps if you select a goal for yourself it would help your child understand this process. Your goals might be as simple as either making dinner or homework a more enjoyable time together. Once you have the goal, you are ready to make a plan. This is similar to drawing a map. You identified the destination; now you need to decide what is the best route for getting there. There may be highways, or towns, or people providing help along the way. You can write these in as things that help you achieve your goals. There also may be obstacles, such as speed limits or traffic jams. You may or may not know in advance what these obstacles will be. You may need to refuel your car en route or stop for refreshments. All of these things can be drawn on the map.

At this time, you may want to use some techniques to check your progress. The simplest techniques we use as adults are those that involve making lists and checking off items. More concrete methods might involve having a toy car move along the route of your map. Teachers often use simple bar graphs with squares of colored construction paper to represent each day of progress. For example, you could show your growth (e.g., successful time together) every day or every week with a cut piece of construction paper to match the height of your positive feelings (one to five inches of paper). The pieces of colored paper may be pasted in sequence onto a big piece of white paper with dates and notes under each piece of paper.

Other Problems

Your child experiences other problems we have not addressed.

Solution

If your child is experiencing other problems which we have not addressed in this section, write them down. Sometimes writing your thoughts on paper and discussing them with your child, the two of you can come up with solutions. Identifying a problem may trigger an idea for a solution. If this process is not helpful, please e-mail us (zentall@purdue.edu or sago@sisna.com). We will give you brief advice and may include your questions in a further revision of this book.

Summary

When using the Learning Station™, we hope your child will have an easier time developing the skills necessary for doing homework independently. The Learning Station™ has been shown to improve work habits in children by helping them organize homework tasks, maintain interest, and increase self-management.

Now we will proceed to step six—Effective Home School Communication. The ideas discussed in this step are extremely important. If your child is having difficulty with homework, there is a good chance that your child is also having trouble with work in school. To provide the best help, parents and teachers must communicate with one another. Step six provides ideas that will help you maintain clear communication with your child's teacher(s).

STEP 6
Effective Home-School Communication

Step 6
Effective Home-School Communication

As we have discussed, one of the most important roles for homework is to form a connection between your family and your child's teachers. We know from experience this connection is often fragile and can be easily broken. This is especially true if your child struggles in school, if you do not understand the goals of assigned homework, or if your goals are different from those of your school (e.g., academic vs. vocational goals).

Interestingly, although parents and teachers agree that communication is often a key to a student's homework success, they often disagree as to how to best share responsibility when problems arise. According to research studies, when communication breaks down, parents and teachers often claim the other has failed in their responsibility for homework.[1] The most frequent complaints from teachers are that parents of students with learning problems infrequently communicated, communicated too late, or failed to follow through.[2] Teachers also expressed that parents do not place as much importance on homework as they should, and they often get defensive or may minimize their child's prob-

lems with homework. We know that parents may not learn about critical homework assignments from their child. The child may have never informed his or her parents that an assignment was due. Nevertheless, it is important for you to understand that teachers expect and encourage parents to take an active role in the learning process and to follow-up with homework problems. Your involvement in school, whatever its form, may communicate to your child that you believe schooling is important.

This step will focus on helping you create an effective system for communicating with your child's teachers about all aspects of school, including homework. Your child has a better chance to succeed if you and your child's teachers develop a means of communicating, work at understanding the situations that appear to cause problems, and develop strategies to solve these problems. Remember, as with communicating with your child, when you communicate with your child's teachers, focus on what needs to be done and how you can help foster a successful process.

The Best Intervention is Prevention

When a new school year starts, attend back-to-school night so you meet with your child's teacher(s). This is an opportunity to get an overview of how the teacher manages his/her class and what will be expected of your child in school. Listen carefully and ask questions. Use this opportunity to understand how and when homework will be assigned, what it will involve, and how you can best communicate with your child's teachers.

We cannot emphasize too strongly the importance of clear, timely communication in regard to homework. If your child has a history of struggling with learning or homework, we urge you to request a brief meeting with your child's teacher specifically to discuss homework. In addition to phone calls, face-to-face meetings, though occurring less frequently, may be your most effective means of developing an efficient communication system. It is critical that these brief meetings are initiated early. To make the most of such meetings, be punctual and respect the teacher's time limits. We also suggest the following:

✎ *Be prepared.* Ask who else may attend the meeting. Organize your thoughts before the conference and write down questions. We suggest you complete the "Parent Profile of My Child" (on the next page) and offer it to the teacher to provide additional insight concerning your thoughts, expectations, and feelings. Bring samples of your child's homework you would like to discuss. Perhaps you have started a homework portfolio that traces your child's progress in specific areas through several grades. Begin the conference with a positive comment, something your child likes about school. Make certain to demonstrate an appreciation for the teacher's efforts. Even in the most conflicted situations, it is important to begin such meetings on a positive note.

✎ *Be a good listener.* Make sure you understand what is being said and take notes. Repeat the elements of what you heard the teacher say. This also gives you time to process the information without becoming defensive.

✎ *Be honest.* If you are struggling, say so. Your child's teacher may be struggling with the very same problems you experience at home. If you feel defensive, remember that you are an advocate for your child. Do not blame anyone for homework problems. Focus on process and solutions.

✎ *Ask questions and accept suggestions.* Mention resources you have explored independently that you believe might be helpful. Ask for your teacher's opinion and reinforce the idea that you know that both of you are on the same team. Most importantly, keep in mind that everyone wants what is best for your child. We suggest you explain *Seven Steps to Homework Success* and introduce this concept to your child's teacher. You might offer the teacher the Special Addendum contained in this workbook. It was prepared especially for teachers to provide them with information about homework practices.

Parent Profile of My Child

Child's Name: _____ Date:_____

Parents' Name(s):_____

My child is interested in_____

_____

_____

My child most enjoys learning about _____

_____

My child least enjoys learning about_____

_____

My child is best doing_____

_____

My child needs the most help with

_____

_____

_____

Things that have helped my child the most in school in the past have been_____

_____

_____

The things I feel least able to help my child with at home are_____

_____

These are the things I would like to know more about concerning homework:

_____

_____

_____

Using Home-Notes to Communicate

Once a homework strategy planning meeting has taken place, further communication between parent and teacher will usually be in writing. Brief notes by the parent or teacher regarding homework will often suffice to alert either one when the child is having a problem. However, for children with chronic homework problems, more frequent, structured reporting may be necessary.

Daily home-notes, sometimes referred to as daily report cards, can be effective for students who experience school problems by improving classroom conduct and academic performance.[3] Such home-notes provide an opportunity for parents to communicate with teachers and more closely monitor their child's daily school progress. Home-notes can vary in detail. Some children may benefit from a daily note containing only the homework assignments given that day and a report on how well previous assignments were completed. Other children may need teachers to prepare brief reports of the child's behavior that day along with homework performance.

Below is an example of a home-note, which tracks behavior, effort, progress, homework, and other information. It can be used either on a daily or weekly basis to keep parents informed of their child's progress.

To encourage the child to improve in school, both parents and teachers need to work with one another on the home note program. They must ensure consistent evaluation by the teacher and regular review by the parents. However, teens and their teachers appear to be less willing to participate in this type of system.

Home-notes can be easily modified to meet each child's needs. Although such notes can be quite helpful, they can also, at times, be quite harmful to the child. Nothing is more demoral-

---

Home-Note

Name: _____   Date: _____

Behavior
___ Positive
___ Satisfactory
___ Occasionally poor
___ Frequently poor

Effort
___ Good, working well
___ Satisfactory
___ Minimal
___ Declining

Progress
___ Satisfactory
___ Unsatisfactory
___ Improving
___ Declining

Homework
___ Thoroughly completed
___ Adequately completed
___ Unprepared

Test Scores
___ Good
___ Average
___ Poor

Work Quality
___ Exceptional
___ Adequate
___ Poor

Friendships
___ Positive
___ Sometimes poor
___ Frequently poor

Teacher's Comments and Signature:

Parent's Comments and Signature:

izing to a child struggling in school than to receive a negative note (or frowny faces) day after day. We suggest that parents and teachers frame information about the child's daily performance in home-notes in as positive a tone as possible. If the child cannot meet the teacher's expectations, perhaps new goals need to be set that are more in line with the child's ability.

Home-notes should be considered a short-term or interim intervention. Your goal should be to move your child toward the use of a daily homework book, day planner, or homework sheet. It can be completed by the child without teacher or parent supervision. It is likely that your child's teachers will already have some type of homework or assignment system in place.

Summary

We cannot over emphasize the importance of communication between parents and teachers about a student's progress. If your child is struggling with homework, there is a good chance your child is also struggling with classwork. It is your role as a parent to understand why your child may be having problems and what you and the school can do to help.

Teachers generally expect and welcome parent input and participation in their child's learning. Due to busy schedules, teachers often have preferred ways to communicate with parents including home-notes, phone calls, e-mail, or scheduled conferences. Parents should try to communicate with teachers as frequently as necessary. Communication should be positive and should focus on problem solving. In certain circumstances, parent-teacher communication may need to be very frequent. Home-notes may be used to provide feedback to all parties regarding the child's school progress.

In step seven we will help you become more aware of what teachers generally consider when assigning homework to students. We will discuss guidelines regarding how homework should be assigned, the content of such assignments, level of difficulty, grading, etc. You may use the information in this section to make recommendations to your child's teachers about homework assignments given to your child.

STEP 7
What Parents Should Know about Homework Assignments

Step 7
What Parents Should
Know About Homework Assignments

Believe it or not, little attention is devoted to the topic of homework in teacher education programs.[1] The homework practices of most teachers are constructed on the job.

When assigning homework teachers must consider at least 3 factors:

- Instructions are clear and understood by all students.

- Assignments are meaningful and within the ability range of all students.

- Assignments will be reviewed, returned, and explained to students.

To some extent, your child's homework problems may stem from the manner in which the teacher assigns, explains, and reviews homework. In this step we will discuss these factors. By becoming familiar with these concepts, you will be able to speak with your child's teachers about how their homework practices could best meet the needs of your child.

Take a moment and complete the "Homework Tips for Teachers Checklist" on the following pages. It was designed to help parents identify the practices their child's teacher uses in assigning homework. This checklist is meant for you, but it may aid you if you choose to offer suggestions to your child's teachers. If you are not sure how to answer a question, check with your child, or your child's teacher, or mark "Don't Know (DK)" in the space provided.

HOMEWORK TIPS FOR TEACHERS CHECKLIST

Making Assignments

____ Yes ____ No ____ DK   1.   Does the teacher provide the purpose of an assignment?

____ Yes ____ No ____ DK   2.   Is the due date provided?

____ Yes ____ No ____ DK   3.   Are materials necessary to successfully complete the assignment recommended?

____ Yes ____ No ____ DK   4.   Are the requirements for good performance explained, including the steps necessary for a long-term assignment or a project?

____ Yes ____ No ____ DK   5.   Is there a system in place for students to obtain help when needed?

____ Yes ____ No ____ DK   6.   Does the teacher provide time at the end of class for students to compare their understanding of homework assignments?

____ Yes ____ No ____ DK   7.   Does the teacher ask students to repeat the assignments in their own words?

____ Yes ____ No ____ DK   8.   Does the teacher provide time for students to begin their assignments in class at joined desks or tables?

____ Yes ____ No ____ DK   9.   Does the teacher require students to re-write or repeat directions before beginning written assignments?

____ Yes ____ No ____ DK   10. Is there a system in place whereby students can ask for help if they do not understand written instructions?

____ Yes ____ No ____ DK   11. Are students taught a system to highlight instructions with colored markers?

____ Yes ____ No ____ DK   12. Does the teacher provide an outline on a weekly or monthly basis of assignments and deadlines?

____ Yes ____ No ____ DK   13. Does the teacher have a system to make certain that students have assignment books, homework planners, or homework buddies to call in the event of problems?

____ Yes ____ No ____ DK   14. Does the teacher offer assignments at the beginning of the class rather than at the end when students may be thinking about recess or lunch?

____ Yes ____ No ____ DK   15. Does the teacher provide verbal instructions with visual prompts (e.g., writing on the blackboard)?

____ Yes ____ No ____ DK   16. Does the teacher offer accommodations for students with learning disabilities or attention problems?

Content of Homework Assignments

____ Yes ____ No ____ DK   17. Do assignments overlap with lessons from the day but provide interest or application rather than just repetition?

____ Yes ____ No ____ DK   18. Does the teacher talk about the purpose of an assignment (e.g., practice)?

____ Yes ____ No ____ DK   19. Does the teacher communicate with you about what is being taught and explain how you can help?

____ Yes ____ No ____ DK   20. Are assignments prioritized so you know which ones to complete if there is limited time?

____ Yes ____ No ____ DK   21. Are some assignments voluntary?

____ Yes ____ No ____ DK   22. Does the teacher allow adaptations for difficulties with handwriting such as the use of a computer?

____ Yes ____ No ____ DK   23. Are some assignments active (e.g., gathering resources, interviewing others, collecting, observing natural phenomena)?

Collecting, Grading, and Returning Assignments

____ Yes ____ No ____ DK   24. Has the teacher provided students with a system to track homework assignments?

____ Yes ____ No ____ DK   25. Are rewards for completing homework as great as the consequences for not completing homework? In other words, does the teacher offer incentives (e.g., extra recess time or reduced homework on a future assignment) when a present assignment is accurate?

____ Yes ____ No ____ DK   26. Do students turn in an excuse sheet when an assignment is missed?

____ Yes ____ No ____ DK   27. Does the teacher allow a certain number of excused homework assignments?

From: Seven Steps to Homework Success by S. Zentall and S. Goldstein (Specialty Press, 1999). Limited copies may be made for personal use.

Once you have completed this checklist, make a list of any unclear questions and seek clarification from your child's teacher. This may be the beginning of an effective homework alliance with the teacher to help your child. Look through the items on the checklist and determine which ideas your child could benefit from if they were used in the classroom.

As you can see from this checklist, teacher practices involving homework can be grouped into three areas: (1) making assignments; (2) content of assignments; and (3) collecting, grading and returning assignments. We will discuss each area below.

Making Assignments

It is important for students to understand the purpose, due date, format, and requirements for good performance when homework is assigned. Interestingly, most teachers assign homework orally with only a minority offering written directions or homework contracts. Further, most teachers assign homework at the end rather than the beginning of class periods.[2] Assigning homework at the end of the period may penalize younger students or students with learning and related attentional problems, whose ability to attend at the end of any lesson is decreased by fatigue or difficulties sustaining attention. It is important that teachers be urged to prepare students for an assignment by communicating to them early in a lesson what the assignment will be and why it is important. It is also imperative that directions are clear and understood by everyone. This is important whether instructions are in written or oral form.

Your child will likely be more successful in returning completed homework if all assignments can be placed in a specific folder and carried to school in this folder. Teachers can also help in this process by having a specific place for homework as school begins. We suggest that at the beginning of the school year, you understand the types of homework assignments that will be given. It would also be helpful if your child's teacher prepares a homework or assignment sheet that can be mimeographed and available on a daily basis.

You may also want to talk to other parents. If a number of students in class are experiencing similar problems with homework, consider organizing a discussion with these parents and then meeting with the teacher.

Content of Assignments

For all students, motivation to complete homework is increased when students find assignments interesting. Boredom has been shown to decrease attention to assignments. Reducing boredom can be achieved by increasing novelty of homework and using materials that are relevant and interesting to your child. For example, rather than computing averages of numbers, an assignment would be more interesting if students computed their school's football team averages for that year in comparison to a prior year.

Active and novel assignments are especially important for children with ADHD. Boredom has been reported by all children, particularly teens, especially when they have been involved in passive activities, such as listening. Less boredom is reported when children engage in hands-on and interactive activities.[3]

In a large survey, elementary teachers offered the following recommendations:[4]

1. Homework should reinforce the school work for that day.

2. Math and reading homework should be given on alternate days.

3. Repetition should be minimal.

4. At-risk students should be allowed to begin homework assignments in class so their performance can be monitored and opportunities can be offered to make certain the assignment is completed correctly.

It is also important that teachers not use assignments as punishment. When assignments become part of a behavior management system, children's attitudes toward these assignments become equally negative. In some cases, this negative attitude spreads to other areas of school. One of the purposes of homework is to foster an enjoyment of working during leisure time.

Estimating the Difficulty of Assignments

Teachers are usually able to assign homework that fits most children's capabilities. For young children, homework should foster positive attitudes toward school and provide a link between home experiences and school learning. For older students, homework should facilitate knowledge acquisition in specific areas. At both age levels, students should learn how to gather and use information and material resources outside the classroom.

However, some assignments will always be too difficult for some children. When assignments vary in difficulty level and students vary in ability, there are several factors to consider. It is important in these circumstances for students to have clear lines of communication and means of obtaining assistance. Homework hotlines or teacher supervised in-class study periods are often beneficial. Teachers are usually willing to alter the length and complexity of homework to accommodate students with learning difficulties or attentional problems.

To assess difficulty, relevance, and length of assignments, we suggest that teachers prepare students for assignments. Students should set up their papers with appropriate headings. In the corner, they should write down how much time the teacher expects the assignment to take. Students are later asked to write down how much time the assignment actually took and rate the assignment based on difficulty and interest. This rating of expected and actual time taken is important feedback. Teachers often underestimate the amount of time it takes to complete homework, especially for students with learning differences.[5]

Reducing Homework

Reduced homework is usually viewed positively by all students. Low priority homework might be dropped or reduced in length, especially for children with ADHD or learning differences. We know that if your child has some control to change the quality or quantity of homework, you may find immediate gains in performance. When middle and secondary students were given rewards of "free homework coupons" for reduced homework if they completed 100% of the week's assignment, their organization and notebook grades improved.[6] Students will also work to improve their behavior if they can earn reduced homework assignments.[7]

Similar gains have been found for students able to leave school early when homework is completed accurately.[8] Some teachers award students free hall passes or homework excuse slips for achieving high homework completion rates. Rewards for completing homework accurately may be especially important for students with a history of school failure. It is important to keep in mind that punishment procedures (e.g., putting students' names on the board) have not been found to produce positive outcomes.

Unfortunately, as children progress into the higher grades, there appears to be an emphasis on the negative consequences for not completing homework rather than on potential positive outcomes. We have found this process leads into a downward spiral of incomplete homework, poor school work, and general dissatisfaction on the student, teacher, and parents' parts.

Collecting, Grading, and Returning Assignments

Homework completion partially depends on the teacher's ability to communicate that completed assignments are valued, expected, and rewarded. It is important to provide some positive outcome for students, especially for children with a history of school or homework difficulties. Furthermore, when feedback is provided quickly and immediately, teachers communicate that homework is a high priority. Feedback also provides students with the motivation necessary to take an active interest in homework.

Typically when elementary school students fail to complete assignments, teachers will talk to them about why the assignment was not completed, will offer assistance, and if the problem persists, communicate with parents.

Summary

This step was included to make you aware of some of the factors teachers must consider when assigning homework. Homework is a rather complex task. Teachers need to consider how they are going to convey the assignment to students, when they should do so, and how they can determine whether student's understand how to do the assignment. In addition, they must consider the content of assignments, including meaningfulness, level of difficulty, and length. Collecting, grading, and providing positive and negative feedback about homework are additional factors teachers must consider.

Parents familiar with these issues will be better prepared to meet with teachers to discuss homework problems. Teachers have little formal training in the techniques of assigning homework. We have prepared a Special Addendum in this workbook, which you may want to give to your child's teacher. It is perforated and easy to remove.

Congratulations! You have completed all seven steps to homework success. Make sure your checklist at the end of the introduction on page four is complete. Now go on to the conclusion to learn how the children living on Elm Street are doing with their homework.

Conclusion
Homework Success in Your Home
and on Elm Street

Conclusion
Homework Success in
Your Home and On Elm Street

If you have reached this point, you have probably just finished reading the entire workbook but have yet to implement all the suggestions. You are probably feeling excited, optimistic, and hopeful. We want you to take this energy, excitement, and hope and translate it into action. This is not always an easy road. It is a road that at times is fraught with twists, turns, and unexpected problems. It is worth pursuing because homework is important and contributes to your child's school and ultimately life success.

After reading this book, we hope that you have a better understanding of the important role of homework in your child's education. You should have a good idea of the skills your child needs to learn and practice in order to manage homework successfully. You should be familiar with the types of things parents can do to promote successful school work and how to solve or avoid common homework problems that may arise in your family. We hope your child found the Learning Station™ to be helpful and that you and your child's teachers have developed effective systems for communication.

As we return to Elm Street, we find every home using a system to develop homework success, yet no two are exactly the same. After reading this book, Mrs. Jones and her son Robert have developed some new ideas that will help Robert complete his homework independently. He has several homework buddies that he keeps in touch with by phone. He also has colored bar graphs to help him chart his own progress, which he reviews with his parents.

Remember Erica, the student with good achievement but low interest in school and homework? Erica's family has diligently worked to help her locate enjoyable, interesting homework activities. They discuss educational interests and learnings at the dinner table. They have developed a system to help Erica take more responsibility for her school work by using a calendar to track assignments. They help Erica break down assignments into steps that she writes on the calendar with dry erase markers. Although Erica would still rather be doing other things, she has accepted the importance of homework and her responsibility in its completion.

Josh and his older sister have learned some skills to help Josh's learning disability. Josh's parents understand that spelling is very difficult for him and are providing additional incentives and rewards. They have also purchased a small, hand held spell checker for Josh.

In the Cunningham household, Emily still completes homework in the kitchen but with the use of the Learning Station™, she finds it easier to stay focused. Andrew still likes to complete homework in front of television, however, he is now watching television during his breaks. His homework contains fewer mistakes, and he has developed a system for checking himself. Susan has agreed with her parents on a specific time to take phone calls and a time when homework must be completed.

Finally, 15-year-old Angela is still completing her homework in her room with the radio blaring and her door closed. Angela and her parents have developed a system by which her parents will be kept apprised of her school progress and performance. As long as she performs at an agreed upon level, she is free to complete homework under her own system.

We are confident that *Seven Steps to Homework Success* has and will provide you with guidance, assistance, and information to help you be a consultant to your child and develop an effective homework alliance. We hope this system will also help homework take a reasonable place in your family life. As always, we welcome your ideas and feedback. We wish you the very best with your children.

Resources

Texts

Davis, L., Sirotowitz, S., & Parker, H.C. (1996). <u>Study strategies made easy: A practical plan for school success</u>. Plantation, FL: Specialty Press.

Dendy, C. (1995). <u>*Teenagers with ADHD: A parents' guide*</u>. Bethesda, MD: Woodbine House.

Goldstein, S., & Goldstein, M. (1992). <u>*Why won't my child pay attention?*</u> New York: Wiley.

Ingersoll, B., & Goldstein, S. (1993). <u>*Attention deficit disorder and learning disability: Realities, myths, and controversial treatments.*</u> New York: Doubleday.

Ingersoll, B., & Goldstein, S. (1995). <u>*Lonely, sad, and angry: A parent's guide to depression in children and adolescence.*</u> New York: Doubleday.

Mather, N., & Goldstein, S. (1998). <u>*Overcoming underachieving: An action guide to helping your child succeed in school.*</u> New York: Wiley.

Mather, N., & Roberts, R. (1996). <u>*Informal assessment and instruction in written language: A practitioner's guide for students with learning disabilities.*</u> New York:Wiley.

Organizations

American Psychiatric Association
1400 K Street, NW
Washington, DC 20005
(202) 682-6000

American Psychological Association
750 First Street, NE
Washington, DC 20002-4242
(202) 336-5500

American Speech-Language-Hearing Association
10801 Rockville Pike
Rockville, MD 20852
(800) 638-8255

National Attention Deficit Disorder Association
9930 Johnnycake Ridge, Suite 3E
Mentor, Ohio 44060
(216) 350-9595

The Orton Dyslexia Society
Chester Building, Suite 382
8600 LaSalle Road
Baltimore, MD 21204

Center for Development and Learning (CDL)
208 S. Tyler St., Suite A
Covington, LA 70433
(504) 893-7777

Children and Adults with Attention Deficit
Disorder (CHADD)
8181 Professional Plaza, Suite 201
Landover, MD 20785
(301) 306-7070
(301) 306-7090 (FAX)
E-mail: national@chadd.org

Council for Exceptional Children (CEC)
and Division for Learning Disabilities (DLD)
1920 Association Drive
Reston, VA 22091-1589
(730) 620-3660 or (800) 328-0272

Council for Learning Disabilities (CLD)
P.O. Box 40303
Overland Park, KS 66204
(913) 492-8755

Educational Resources Information Center
(ERIC)
Eric Clearinghouse on Disabilities
and Gifted Education
1920 Association Drive
Reston, VA 22091
(800) 328-0272

Franklin Learning Resources
122 Burrs Road
Mt. Holley, NY 08060
(800) 525-9673
(markets a variety of electronic aides,
including spell checkers)

Learning Disabilities Association (LDA)
4156 Library Road
Pittsburgh, PA 15234
(412) 341-1515

National Alliance for the Mentally Ill
(800) 950-NAMI

National Alliance for the Mentally Ill -
Children and Adolescent Network
(703) 524-7600

National Center for Learning Disabilities
(NCLD)
381 Park Avenue, Suite 1420
New York, NY 10016
(212) 545-7510

National Center for Law and Learning Disabilities
(NCLLD)
P.O. Box 368
Cabin John, MD 20818
(301) 469-8308

National Foundation for Depressive Illness
(800) 248-4344

National Information Center for Children and
Youth with Disabilities (NICHCY)
P.O. Box 1492
Washington, DC 20013-1492
(800) 695-0285

National Right to Read Foundation
Box 490
The Plans, VA 20198
(800) 468-8911

Parents' Educational Resource Center (PERC)
1660 S. Amphlett Blvd., Suite 200
San Mateo, CA 94402-2508
(415) 655-2410

Recordings for the Blind and Dyslexic
20 Roszel Road
Princeton, NJ 08540
(800) 221-4792

Tourette's Syndrome Association
4240 Bell Blvd.
Bayside, NY 11361-2874
(718) 224-2999

Books, Newsletters, Videos, and Training Programs for Children with Special Needs
A.D.D. WareHouse
300 N.W. 70th Ave., Suite 102
Plantation, Florida 33317
(800) 233-9273
www.addwarehouse.com

Online Homeowork Help Sites

If the library is closed and a student needs to find resources, there are several reference resources online. Here are a few:

Information Please, www.infoplease.com .
Contains an assortment of searchable almanacs.

www.schoolwork.org. This is a site for seventh grade and higher. Students can e-mail a librarian for assistance.
Kids Click! sunsite.berkeley.edu/KidsClick!
This is a searchable and comprehensive directory of internet resources for kids.

www.nosweat.com. This site contains Homework Central Jr. for grades 1-6, Homework Central for grades 7 and up and Encyclopedia Central for college and above.

Other Internet Sites

American School Directory, http://
www.asd.com. Lists all K-12 schools in U.S.

CHADD, http://www.chadd.org. Information on ADD/ADHD, children and adults.

Council for Exceptional Children, Division for Learning Disabilities, http://
curry.edschool.virginia.edu/-sjs5d/dld (CEC = www.cec.sped.org). Geared toward educators, good links; see parent site.

LD Online, http://www.ldonline.org. Covers all aspects of LD; clearinghouse.

LD Resources (was Poor Richard's Publishing), http://www.ldresources.com. Many subjects; learning disabilities software.

Learning Disabilities Association of America, http://www.idanati.org. Information, resources, local, state chapters.

National ADD Association, http://
www.add.org. Medications, support groups, links.

National Adult Literacy and Learning Disabilities Center (NALLDC), http://novel.nifl.gov/nalldtop.htm. Publications and hot topics about LD and adult literacy.

National Center for Learning Disabilities (NCLD), http://www.ncld.org. Information on all aspects of LD; resources, links.

International Dyslexia Association (was Orton Dyslexia Society), http://interdys.org. Information on dyslexia; research, legislation, state chapters.

One A.D.D. Place, http://
www.greatconnect.com/oneaddplace. Checklists, resources, products, conferences, more for ADD/ADHD.

Parents Educational Resource Center (PERC), http://www.perc-schwabfdn.org. Resources by subject and type; services, publications, links.

Parents of Gifted/Learning Disabled Children, http://www.geocities.com/athens. Information on gifted/LD children; parent, child, and educator support.

Matrix Parent Network, http://marin.org/edu/matrix/index.html. Support for parents of children with disabilities.

National Information Center for Children and Youth with Disabilities (NICHY), http://www.nichy.org. Information on all disabilities and related issues.

Parents Helping Parents, http://www.php.com. Resources, links, technology.

Recordings for the Blind and Dyslexic, http://www.rfbd.org. Information on materials on audiotapes and digital formats.

References

Step 1

1. Baumgartner, D., Bryan, T., Donahue, M., & Nelson, C. (1993). Thanks for asking: Parent comments about homework, tests, and grades. Exceptionality, 4, 177-185.
2. Cooper, H. (1989). Synthesis of reearch on homework. Educational Leadership, 47, 85-91.
3. Epstein, J. L. (1988). Homework practices, achievements, and behaviors of elementary school students. (Report No. 26). Baltimore, MD: Johns Hopkins University, Center for Research on Elementary and Middle Schools.
4. Cooper, H., & Nye, B. (1994). Homework for students with learning disabilities: The implications of research for policy and practice. Journal of Learning Disabilities, 27, 470-479.
5. Cooper, H., & Nye, B. (1994). Homework for students with learning disabilities: The implications of research for policy and practice. Journal of Learning Disabilities, 27, 470-479.
6. Cooper, H., & Nye, B. (1994). Homework for students with learning disabilities: The implications of research for policy and practice. Journal of Learning Disabilities, 27, 470-479.
7. Miller, D. L., & Kelley, M. L. (1991). Interventions for improving homework performance: A critical review. School Psychology Quarterly, 6, 174-185.
8. Cooper, H., & Nye, B. (1994). Homework for students with learning disabilities: The implications of research for policy and practice. Journal of Learning Disabilities, 27, 470-479.
9. Murphy, J., & Decker, K. (1990). Homework use at the high school level: Implications for principals. NASSP Bulletin, 74, 40-43.
10. Epstein, M. H., Polloway, E. A., Foley, R. M., & Patton, J. R. (1993). Homework: A comparison of teachers' and parents' perceptions of the problems experienced by students identified as behaviorally disordered, learning disabeled, and non-disabeled. Remedial and Special Education, 14, 40-50.
10. Salend, S. J., and Schliff, J. (1988). The many dimensions of homework. Academic Therapy, 23, 397-403.
11. Keith, T. Z., & Cool, V. A. (1992). Testing models of school learning: Effects of quality of instrction, motivation, adademic coursework, and homework on academic achievement. School Psychology Quarterly, 7, 207-226.
12. Cooper, H., & Nye, B. (1994). Homework for students with learning disabilities: The implications of research for policy and practice. Journal of Learning Disabilities, 27, 470-479.
13. Polloway, E. A., Epstein, M. H., Bursuck, W. D., Madhavi, J., & Cumblad, C. (1994). Homework practices of general education teachers. Journal of Learning Disabilities, 27, 500-509.
14. Nicholls, J. G., McKenzie, M., & Shufro, J. (1994). Schoolwork, homework, life's work: The experience of students with and without learning disabilities. Journal of Learning Disabilities, 27, 562-569.
15. Kay, P. J., Fitzgerald, M., Paradee, C., & Mellencamp, A. (1994). Making homework work at home: The parents' perspective. Journal of Learning Disabilities, 27, 550-561.
16. Murphy, J., & Decker, K. (1990). Homework use at the high school level: Implications for principals. NASSP Bulletin, 74, 40-43.
17. Bryan, T., & Nelson, C. (1994). Doing homework: Perspectives of elementary and junior high school students. Journal of Learning Disabilities, 27, 488-499.
18. Larson, R. W., & Richards, M. H. (1991). Boredom in the middle school years: Blaming schools versus blaming students. American Journal of Education, 99, 418-443
19. Murphy, J., & Decker, K. (1990). Homework use at the high school level: Implications for principals. NASSP Bulletin, 74, 40-43.

20. Baumgartner, D., Bryan, T., Donahue, M., & Nelson, C. (1993). Thanks for asking: Parent comments about homework, tests, and grades. Exceptionality, 4, 177-185.
21. Milkent, M. M., & Roth, W.M. (1989). Enhancing student achievement through computer generated homework. Journal of Research in Science Teaching, 26, 567-573.
22. Murphy, J., & Decker, K. (1989). Teachers' use of homework in high schools. Journal of Educational Research, 82, 261-269.

Step 3

1. Bryan, T., & Nelson, C. (1994). Doing homework: Perspectives of elementary and junior high school students. Journal of Learning Disabilities, 27, 488-499. See also: Cooper, H. & Nye, B., (1994). Homework for students with learning disabilities: The implications of research for policy and practice. Journal of Learning Disabilities, 27, 470-479.
2. Jenson, W. R., Sheridan, S. M., Olympia, D., & Andrews, D. (1994). Homework and students with learning disabilities and behavior disorders: A practical, parent-based approach. Journal of Learning Disabilities, 27, 538-548.
3. Bryan, T., & Nelson, C. (1994), Doing homework: Perspectives of elementary and junior high school students. Journal of Learning Disabilities, 27, 488-499.
4. Abikoff, H., Courtney, M. E., Szeibel, P. J., & Koplewicz, H. S. (1996). The effects of auditory stimulation on the arithmetic performance of children with ADHD and nondisabled children. Journal of Learning Disabilities, 29, 238-246.
5. Cooper, H., & Nye, B., (1994). Homework for students with learning disabilities: The implications of research for policy and practice. Journal of Learning Disabilities, 27, 470-479.
6. Miller, D. L., & Kelley, M. L. (1991). Interventions for improving homework performance: A critical review. School Psychology Quarterly, 6, 174-185.
8. Zentall, S. S., Moon, S. M., Grskovic, J., Hall, A. M., & Stormont-Spurgin, M. (1999). Learning characteristics of boys with giftedness and/or attention deficit/hyperactivity disorder. Manuscript submitted for publication.
8. Reavis, G. H. (1953). The animal school. Educational Forum, 17, 141.
9. Jones, C. B. (1994). Attention Deficit Disorder: Strategies for School Age Children. San Antonio, TX: Communication Skill Builders: A Division of the Psychological Corporation.
10. Landers, M. E. (1984). Helping the LD Child with Homework: Ten Tips. Academic Therapy, 20, 209-215.

Step 4

1. Murphy, J., & Decker, K. (1990). Homework use at the high school level: Implications for principals. NASSP Bulletin, 74, 40-43.
2. Bryan, T., & Nelson, C. (1994). Doing homework: Perspectives of elementary and junior high school students. Journal of Learning Disabilities, 27, 488-499.
3. Polloway, E. A., Epstein, M. H., & Foley, R. (1992). A comparison of the homework problems of students with learning disabilities and non-handicapped students. Learning Disabilities: Research and Practice, 7, 203-209.
4. Salend, S. J., and Schliff, J. (1988). The many dimensions of homework. Academic Therapy, 23, 397-403.
5. Zentall, S. S., Falkenberg, S. D., & Smith, L. B. (1985). Effects of color stimulation on the copying performance of attention-problem adolescents. Journal of Abnormal Child Psychology, 13, 501-511.
6. Zentall, S. S. (1993). Research on the educational implications of attention deficit hyperactivity disorder. Exceptional Children, 60, 143-153.
7. Rubinstein, R. A., & Brown, R. T. (1981). An evaluation of the validity of the diagnositc category of ADD. American Journal of Orthopsychiatry, 54, 398-414.

Step 5

1. Somervill, J. W., Warnberg, L.S., & Bost, D. E. (1973). Effects of cubicles versus increased stimulation on task performance by first-grade males perceived as distractible and nondistractible. Journal of Special Education, 7, 169-175.
2. Berlyne, D. E. (1960). Conflict, arousal, and curiosity. New York: McGraw-Hill.
3. Hall, A. M., & Zentall, S. S. (1999). The effects of a learning station on the completion and accuracy of math homework for middle school students. Manuscript submitted for publication.
4. Carver, C. S., & Scheier, M. F. (1981). Attention and self-regulation: A control therapy approach to human behavior . New York: Springer Press.
5. Zentall, S. S., Hall, A. M., & Lee, D. L. (1998). Attentional focus of students with hyperactivity during a word-search task. Journal of Abnormal Child Psychology, 26, 335-343.

Step 6

1. Jayanthi, M., Nelson, J. S., Sawyer, V., Bursuck, W. D., & Epstein, M. H. (1995). Homework-communication problems among parents, general education, and special education teachers: An exploratory study. Remedial and Special Education, 16, 102-116.
2. Epstein, M. H., Polloway, E. A., Buck, G. H., Bursuck, W. D., Wissinger, L. M., Whitehouse, F., & Jayanthi, M. (1995). Homework-related communication problems: Perspectives of general education teachers. Learning Disabilities Research and Practice, 12, 221-227.
3. Kelly, M.L. (1990). School-home notes: Promoting children's classroom success. New York: Guilford.

Step 7

1. Jenson, W. R., Sheridan, S. M., Olympia, D., & Andrews, D. (1994). Homework and students with learning disabilities and behavior disorders: A practical, parent-based approach. Journal of Learning Disabilities, 27, 538-548.
2. Murphy, J., & Decker, K. (1989). Teachers' use of homework in high schools. Journal of Educational Research, 2, 261-269.
3. Larson, R. W., & Richards, M. H. (1991). Boredom in the middle school years: Blaming schools versus blaming students. American Journal of Education, 99. 418-443
4. Cooper, H., & Nye, B. (1994). Homework for students with learning disabilities: The implications of research for policy and practice. Journal of Learning Disabilities, 27, 470-479.
5. Bryan, T., & Sulivan-Burstein, K. (1997). Homework. Teaching Exceptional Children, July/August, 32-37.
6. Cooper, H., & Nye, B. (1994). Homework for students with learning disabilities: The implications of research for policy and practice. Journal of Learning Disabilities, 27, 470-479.
7. McLaughlin, T. F., Swain, J. C., Brown, M., & Fielding, L. (1986). The effects of academic consequences on the inappropriate social behavior of special education middle school students. Techniques: A Journal for Remedial Education and Counseling, 2, 310-316.
8. Miller, D. L., & Kelley, M. L. (1991). Interventions for improving homework performance: A critical review. School Psychology Quarterly, 6, 174-185.

Index

Special Addendum
A Brief Teacher's Guide to Homework

The following section was prepared as a guide for your child's teacher(s). These pages can be easily removed from this book and provided to teachers who may be interested in reviewing empirical research about homework.

Special Addendum
A Brief Teacher's Guide to Homework

Sidney S. Zentall, Ph.D. and Sam Goldstein, Ph.D.

From: Seven Steps to Homework Success by S. Zentall and S. Goldstein (Specialty Press, 1999).
Limited copies may be made for personal use.

Children differ significantly in their attitudes about homework and the methods they use to complete it. Teachers also differ in the strategies, reasons for, and types of homework they assign. This *Brief Teacher's Guide to Homework* comes from *Seven Steps to Homework Success* authored by psychologists and educators, Drs. Sydney S. Zentall and Sam Goldstein (Specialty Press, 1999). This seven step guide provides a research-based program and set of strategies to improve children's ability to collect, complete, and return homework successfully. One of the unique aspects about this program is the use of the Learning Station™, a free-standing, three-sided panel found to increase independent homework completion. As a special addendum to *Seven Steps to Homework Success*, Drs. Zentall and Goldstein have provided a teacher's guide to homework and suggested that copies be provided to teachers. Hopefully, the information within this guide will be helpful.

Difficulties with completing homework have been documented for more than a fourth of students in general education classrooms and for more than half of students with learning disabilities.[1] Children with learning problems often consider homework another opportunity to fail, and so they resist. Children with ADHD may resist homework, especially when it involves work sheets or repetition of daily lessons. Even for gifted students, homework can be unpleasant, especially when teachers feel that children who can't do the basics (e.g., worksheets, practice tasks) should not be provided with more challenging assignments.

In spite of these student-centered problems, we know that there are benefits to be derived from homework. Homework is a cost-effective way to deliver instruction, which increases in importance as children move into junior and senior high school. Some of the benefits are across grade levels, such as learning how to gather and use information and material resources outside the classroom. There are other expected benefits that depend on the age of the student. For elementary aged students, homework should foster positive attitudes toward school and provide a link between home experiences and school learning. At this age, students need high levels of feedback and/or supervision, so they can practice their assignments correctly. For example, at the elementary level, in-class study produced better achievement, probably because of the increased amount of feedback from adults or peers during study time compared with homework.[2] Homework with parental feedback produced better test scores for fourth through sixth grade elementary students than similar classes without homework .[3]

For students in middle and high school, homework should facilitate knowledge acquistion in specific areas. At this age, there are greater benefits from time engaged in practicing and thinking about school work. These benefits do not appear to depend upon immediate supervision or feedback. The average high schooler outperformed almost three quarters of peers in a nonhomework class as measured by standardized tests—with junior high students achieving half that gain.[4]

We know that the benefits from homework are the greatest for students who complete the most homework and who do so correctly. Students who are older or more skilled are more likely to perform homework correctly. Thus, students who devote time to homework are probably on a path to improved achievement, but with them on that path is higher quality instruction, greater achievement motivation, and better skill levels. Educators have some influence over each of these areas. But before we address the role you can play, what resources can you call upon?

What Resources are Available?

Little attention is devoted to the topic of homework in teacher education programs.[5] Homework practices are constructed by teachers on-the-job. Furthermore, the vast majority of all teachers (two thirds) reported that there were no structures to assist them as they implemented homework procedures. That is, "homework is largely uncoordinated and unmanaged at the district, the school, or the department level"(p. 42).[6] Only about a third of school districts had a homework policy. For most of the school districts with a policy, it was not a required policy, and there were modifications for students with disabilities.[7] Policies for students with disabilities are particularly important because many of these students receive instruction in a variety of

settings. Administrators need to support teachers by coordinating the amounts of homework they receive and perhaps the days on which this homework is scheduled. Homework should be similar, at least in time required, for those students in special settings as for those in inclusive settings.

For the majority of school districts with a homework policy, there were also guidelines for the roles of parents: (p. 484)[8]

1. Provide space and consequences for completed work.

2. Monitor time allocation and task completion.

3. Assist children in studying for tests.

4. Tutor children in specific skills.

5. Provide children with additional enrichment activities.

Such school guidelines may be useful, especially for those of you who haven't communicated your expectations about homework to your parents. Only about a third of parents reported they knew the homework rules for their children's schools.[9]

In summary, we believe it is helpful for you to have some school or district ground rules from which to work. Perhaps communicating with your administrators will clarify some unwritten or written policies regarding homework, which will be useful for you as a starting point. Without this input and in the absence of training, we know that decisions about homework are primarily made by you, and these decisions often fall back on tradition or local practice.

We will provide you with a number of empirically-based strategies in the information to follow. The checklist on the following page might serve as the basis for a discussion with your administrators.

POSITIVE ADMINISTRATOR HOMEWORK POLICIES

____Yes ____ No   1.   Have you developed a standard, school-wide style for homework headings to reduce the need to teach students how to head their papers every year?

____ Yes ____ No   2.   Do you hold after-school homework programs for small groups of students with recurrent incompletion of homework?

____ Yes ____ No   3.   Do you have a flexible homework policy that lists possible adaptations for students with disabilities?

____ Yes ____ No   4.   Do you encourage your elementary teachers to assign homework that is active and involves the whole family?

____ Yes ____ No   5.   Do you encourage your secondary teachers to provide incentives for turning in homework?

____ Yes ____ No   6.   Do you monitor teachers' use of routine places for assigning, collecting, and returning homework?

____ Yes ____ No   7.   Do you have a flexible grading policy that provides adaptations for children with disabilities?

____ Yes ____ No   8.   Have you communicated your homework and grading policies to parents?

____ Yes ____ No   9.   Have you monitored the implementation of those policies?

____ Yes ____ No   10. Do you ask your teachers to communicate their homework and grading policies to parents?

____ Yes ____ No   11. Do you coordinate the scheduling of homework among the different subject areas or teachers?

____ Yes ____ No   12. Have you provided inservice education or faculty discussion related to policies and practices?

What Can Teachers Do?

In general, teachers' problems with homework can be grouped into three areas: 1) problems in making assignments, (2) problems in the meaningfulness, difficulty, and length of assignments, and (3) problems with getting homework returned. These problems are addressed in the following sections. Problems in getting students to complete homework are experienced by all educators, but teachers of students with special needs have even more difficulty.

Making Assignments

When you make assignments, clear instructions are important. The following checklist will help you evaluate your practices related to making assignments.

Do you provide the...

_____ Yes _____ No   1.   purpose of the assignment?

_____ Yes _____ No   2.   date due?

_____ Yes _____ No   3.   format required or suggested?

_____ Yes _____ No   4.   necessary materials and other resources (dictionaries, indexes), which includes the types of assistance students can receive from others and how to obtain assistance?

_____ Yes _____ No   5.   requirements for good performance, which includes steps in a complex task?

In addition to these points, instruction-related, there are several things to consider in the way you make assignments. Reports from high school teachers indicate that the majority of them assign homework orally; only a minority of teachers use written directions or homework contracts. Furthermore, the majority of you assign homework at the end of the class period and less than a quarter of you assign it at the beginning of the period.[10] Assigning homework at the end of the period may penalize young students and students with learning, attentional, or emotional problems. Their ability to attend at the end of any task is decreased by difficulties sustaining attention. When you make assignments, prepare your students by communicating to them early in the lesson what the assignment will be and why it is important.

Secondly, you will have better outcomes if you make sure the directions are clear. This is particularly important when the directions are verbal. When the directions are written, there are a number of other ways to make sure they are understood (see box on following page).

Do you help your students understand verbal instructions?

____ Yes ____ No   1.   Do you provide time at the end of giving an assignment for students to talk and compare their understandings?

____ Yes ____ No   2.   Do you ask for students to volunteer to repeat the assignment in their own words?

____ Yes ____ No   3.   Do you provide a period of time for students to begin their assignments in class while working with others at joined desks or tables?

Do you help your students understand written instructions?

____ Yes ____ No   1.   Do you provide magic markers (with overlays for text books) for students to highlight or underline key words in the directions or mathematical symbols on a worksheet?

____ Yes ____ No   2.   Do you have students rewrite or state out loud the directions before beginning (especially when they need to write an essay)?

Furthermore, a homework or assignment sheet can be prepared, mimeographed, and available to use on a daily basis. The use of assignment/calendar books has become increasingly popular. You can help all students with their assignments by requiring the use of specific colored folders or assignment books while carrying assignments to and from school.[11] Students can also have specific places to store homework in their desks or lockers. Where problems persist for one or more students you could organize groups to discuss how different children manage their assignments and what problems or successes they experience. The bottom line is that your students, especially those with disabilities, require a well-defined system to collect and carry home homework assignments.

Content and Length

For students to be motivated to complete assignments, the content of those assignments should be meaningful, at a moderate difficulty level, and not too long or repetitive. In reality, the most frequent types of assignments are unfinished classwork and practice tasks.[12] In high school settings, where assignments could be more varied and address the higher order skills of application and creativity (e.g., essays, book reports, research reports, projects), the range of homework assigned is actually narrower. Teachers usually assign two types of homework: (1) textbooks with questions and (2) worksheets.[13] The types of homework that many teachers felt were helpful, especially at the older age levels, may contribute to students' perceptions that their homework assignments are boring.

Boredom has been shown to decrease attention to assignments contribute to negative evaluation of school, and to higher drop out rates.[14] Boredom plays a significant role in reducing student motivation and plays an even a greater role at older age levels, as self-reported by students.[15] The effects of boredom on performance are that students complete less work and it is completed less accurately. For example, one study found that approximately half of the high school students did not finish their practice types of assignments. Less than half the students achieved expected accuracy rates of 80 to 100% correct for the work that was completed.[16]

There are many of ways to reduce boredom. A large sample of your colleagues across grade levels recommended the following:[17]

> 1. Homework should reinforce or extend the school work for that day.
>
> 2. Math and reading homework should be given on alternate days.
>
> 3. Repetition should be kept at a minimum.
>
> 4. At risk students should be allowed to begin homework assignments in class, so performance could be monitored and opportunities to self-correct could be given.

Some of these recommendations address repetition of work and its contribution to boredom. Where repetition is necessary, we recommend assigning practice tasks and repetition at spaced intervals of time. For example, editing of work can be done at a later time. Similarly, boredom can be reduced by increasing the variety of as-

signments and methods of practice. For example, fast paced computer programs with multiple choice questions in comparison to traditional homework tasks have been found to actually raise the potential of students over what was predicted from their standardized test scores.[18] The need for greater variety of assignments was expressed by one parent who commented, "In social studies and science he gets 'fun' projects, but the math teacher works right out of the book. It's really turned my son off" (p. 183).[19]

For all students motivation to complete homework is also increased by altering the meaningfulness of assignments. If the assignment is interesting and relevant to that age level or there are elements of choice in the assignment, there will be higher rates of completion. Fewer homework problems are experienced by children who see how school work relates to their own skills or experiences.[20] Sometimes interesting materials are those that are relevant to a specific locale. For example, rather than having students compute averages of unrelated numbers, an assignment would be more interesting by having students compute their school's football team's current averages in comparison to a prior year.

Finally, today's view of education increasingly focuses on students creating their own understanding through experience and discovery (e.g., to develop their own position on the question of why dinosaurs became extinct). Some teachers assign children the task of thinking up many different ways to solve several math problems. Even though you may be less familiar with these types of divergent thinking homework tasks, such creative and experiential tasks can be quite enjoyable for your students.

Assignments that are active and novel are especially important for students with ADHD and for adolescents, who report more boredom in their assignments. The highest rates of boredom have been reported by all adolescents during more passive activities (e.g., social studies, listening) and lower rates were reported during hands-on and interactive activities (e.g., music, art, gym, lab work, discussion). [21]

The last factor, related to the content of the assignment and to the likelihood that homework will be completed, is the difficulty of assignments. For students to independently complete an assignment, they must have achieved a moderate level of understanding during class.[22] If students do not understand the material, they will be frustrated while attempting to complete their homework. Where assignments vary in difficulty level and students vary in ability, you need to consider whether the child can obtain needed assistance either at home or in school. In some schools, telephone hotlines are teacher-staffed during the evening hours or there are teacher supervised in-class study periods. This is especially important at younger grade levels.

To control difficulty, you might consider how length contributes to the importance of an assignment. Homework can be reduced in length to accommodate slower students, without changing your grading times. In contrast, adding length can create a paperwork burden on you and doesn't necessarily increase the educational importance of the assignment. Simply giving students more of the same has questionable educational value. Furthermore, adding length to assignments makes them especially difficult for students with learning or attentional problems.

With all these suggestions, if you are still unsure how your students are responding to your assignments in terms of perceived difficulty, meaningfulness, and length, prepare your students for an assignment by having them set up their paper with appropriate headings. In the corner, write down how much time you expect the assignment to take.[23] The students will later write down how much time the assignment actually took and a rating of perceived difficulty or interest, using happy/sad faces or numbers. This rating of expected and actual time taken is important because educators often underestimate the amount of time it will take to complete homework, especially for students with disabilities. [24]

ASSIGNMENT FORMAT AND PRIORITY

Student Name_____

Subject Area_____

Date Due_____

Expected Time for Assignment_____Actual time

spent?_____

Teacher's Assignment Priority	High	Medium	Low
Student's Difficulty Rating:	Easy	Medium	Difficult
Student's Interest Rating:	High	Medium	Low

Completing Assignments

Problems in getting students to complete homework are experienced by all educators, but teachers of special needs students have even more difficulty. For both groups, completion of homework depends on your ability to communicate that completed assignments are valued, expected, and rewarded.[25]

To make sure the assignment is valued, you need to first ask yourself the question—is this an important assignment and why? When this question is answered, you can give priority scores to homework assignments. This will also help you decide what the consequence or incentives will be for each assignment. Homework completion needs to provide some positive outcome for students, especially for children who have a history of school or homework difficulties. There are several options to improve the cost/benefit ratio.

Feedback. For your purposes, homework with feedback is used to identify problems individual students may have in independent work (i.e., to evaluate teaching and learning). When homework is returned with written or oral feedback, it communicates high priority.[26] In support of this conclusion, assignments with teacher feedback produced gains in achievement over those assignments with no feedback.[27] Room-helpers, whether they are parents, high-school aides, or university undergraduate education majors can help you with these feedback tasks.

Sometimes feedback that just communicates how much homework was completed is sufficient to motivate children to perform better. That is, teaching students how to graph percent of homework completed per day using colorful bar graphs has been successful in improving homework completion.[28] For example, the color green can be used communicate completed work and yellow for late work.

Grading homework. Homework is used more often to evaluate student effort and progress. You accomplish this purpose by assigning grades to homework. Even though some researchers believe that homework should <u>not</u> be viewed as an opportunity to test, grading homework is typically used, especially at the secondary level.[29] The majority of high school teachers graded 81 to 100% of their assignments, mostly by themselves and by teacher aids.[30]

Middle and high school teachers more than elementary school teachers reported that recording performance in a grade book was helpful.[31] At the high school level, almost all the teachers computed the scores into the semester grades of students. The homework part of the overall grade was an average of 20% of the semester grade. Some teachers counted homework as much as 40% or more of the semester grade.

When homework is this important to you, explain to your students the contribution of homework to their grades and the effects of 0s on their grades. This can be done by teaching them the principles of averaging and how extreme scores influence the summative scores. To offset the influence of external circumstances that occur for all children, many teachers allow students to drop their lowest grade(s).

Although most teachers say that there are school grading policies, less than a quarter of teachers reported that there were policies related to the grading of students with special needs.[32] Elementary teachers are more likely than high school teachers to adjust evaluation standards for students with disabilities.[33] Some of the ways to adjust evalution when grading homework of students with disabilities include contracting students for a certain amount of work to equal a specific grade or pass/fail criteria.[34] In addition, the Individual Educational Plan (IEP) can be used as the basis of a grade (e.g., an IEP may require a 90% accuracy level with a range of 86 to 93% to equal a letter grade of B).

Additionally, assignments can be graded for students with special needs to reflect differences between an assignment accommodation and an assignment change. An educator makes an assignment accommodation by breaking down a larger task into smaller tasks spaced out over a period of time with checkpoints. Similarly, an educator could assign fewer problems to be completed, but these problems would still represent the full range of curriculum content. In these accommodations, the content does not change; only the amount of material, the time, or some modification of task input or response is changed. Additional examples of accommodations could be: (a) follows homework directions when directions are written or are highlighted, (b) completes assignments accurately when there is an opportunity to discuss the assignment with a buddy following the teacher's instructions, (c) completes homework assignments accurately with the aid of a computer.

An assignment change involves alterations of the information, curriculum content, or lesson objective. If the lesson objective is solving math story problems, then reading the problem to the child or allowing the child to use a calculator does not represent a change of lesson objective. However, if the objective is math calculation and the child computes math problems using a calculator, then a change of lesson objective has been made. Here checking math calculations with a calculator would be reinforcing to the child after the completion of a certain number of problems; it does not involve changing the lesson objective. Similarly, if the lesson objective is understanding reading, demonstration of this objective could involve (a) drawing a sequence of cartoons showing the story events, (b) verbally describing or typing the sequence of these events, or (c) play acting the events. However, if the teacher is working on story construction (language), than a change of objectives would occur if you allowed the child to draw a series of cartoons or act out the events. Verbally describing or typing the story events would not

be a change in the lesson objective.

When a change in the lesson objective has been made, it is more difficult for teachers to justify giving students an A for work that does not meet the objective of the lesson and is clearly not comparable to other students in class. When task changes are made, a student's recommended maximum grade would be a B, not an A.[35] However, even for students for whom a task change has been made and who put forth reasonable effort, a minimum grade would be a D.

Turning in and Returning

When students failed to complete assignments, elementary level teachers (more than secondary level teachers) reported [36] that it was most helpful to:

✎ Talk to students about why assignments were not completed.

✎ Assist students in completing assignments (peer tutors, aids, checking more frequently).

✎ Give fewer assignments or cut the assignment length.

✎ Make adaptations in assignments (alternative formats).

✎ Require parent signatures on assignments.

✎ Recommend homework strategies for home use.

✎ Send notes home.

There are several additional general suggestions we recommend to improve homework completion.

Establish and Reinforce Routines. Assignments are more likely to be returned to school when you have a scheduled time and a routine place for assigning, collecting, and returning homework. Responsibilities related to collecting and filing homework can be assigned as rotating roles to classroom members. Roles and responsibilities are especially important for students who have difficulty completing or turning in homework.

Students with ADHD report that they do their homework but can't find it when it is time to turn it in.[37] Parents confirm this when they go to school to help clean out their children's desks and find many assignments that the child did not turn in. An older peer or classroom buddy can be provided to help students with these placement and retrieval tasks.

Offer Reduced Homework as an Incentive. We also know that if students have some control to reduce the quantity of homework, there may be immediate gains in performance. Reduced homework is usually viewed positively by all students. When middle and secondary students were given "free homework" coupons for reduced homework if they completed their week's assignment, it improved their organization and notebook grades.[38] Middle school students with behavioral problems will also work to improve their behavior if they can get reduced homework.[39] It is also possible to use reduced length or certain types of assignments as rewards to work for. The following box is a constructive example of this.

BASEBALL AND HOMEWORK

We knew of one teacher who used a baseball game as a type of whole class behavior management. When problems arised during the day, the teacher called a strike. These were usually whole class noise levels or percentages of the class failing to turn in assignments, etc.

At the opposite end, positive comments, behavior, or performance were called home runs. A run would cancel a strike.

If three strikes were accumulated, several outcomes were possible: (1) students would have an in-class test rather than a take-home, (2) students would have a closed book test, rather than an open book/notes test, (3) students would have a pop quiz, etc.

Use School Privileges as Incentives. Similar gains were found for elementary level students, who got to leave school 15 minutes early if they completed their homework the night before at an accuracy level of 80%.[40] Some teachers award students free hall passes or homework excuse slips for achieving higher homework completion rates.

Rewards for completing homework accurately may be especially important for students with histories of school failure. For example, students with LD performed better on classroom quizzes when they had practiced homework spelling words with rates of 90% correct and 90% completed in exchange for tokens. These tokens were used for free time, computer, or library time.[41]

RAIN CHECK

Work must be handed in within ONE

week of due date.

Assignment was_____

Due date was_____

Today's date is_____

Signed by (teacher's name)_____

HALL PERMIT

Today's date is_____

Signed by (teacher's

name)_____

Eliminate Punishment. As a general rule, do not use assignments as punishment.[42] When assignments become a part of a behavior management system, students' attitudes toward these assignments will become equally negative. This attitude could spread. One of the purposes of homework is to foster an enjoyment of working during leisure time. If students find that their assignments are intended as punishment, then the proposed benefits from homework will not be realized.

Teachers are generally aware that punishment procedures (e.g., putting students' names on the board, reducing grades) do not produce positive outcomes.[43] Even so, at the secondary level, there appears to be a greater emphasis on the negative consequences for not completing homework than on the potenial for homework to provide positive outcomes. Although these teachers rated lowering grades as more helpful than did elementary teachers, when one middle school reading teacher actually evaluated her practices [44] she arrived at a very different conclusion. Susan Davis attempted to correct her classroom problem of students not completing homework by punishing the behavior. That is, she gave detentions when students did not turn in their homework, which overburdened the discipline system. Then, she began to count homework as a part of the final grade. That solution resulted in many students with failing grades. Finally, when it was clear that punishment was not the answer, she found that giving students an excuse sheet for noncompletion of homework almost eliminated homework as a factor in failing grades. She used an excuse sheet—similar to the one we redesigned here. When students did not complete their homework, they filled out an excuse sheet to explain why the homework was not done. After using the sheet for one term, more than 60% of the 140 students raised their grades. It was especially helpful for students whose homework grades were below 50%. Writing down the reason for the excuse may have made students think about the basis of their excuse without needing to also defend themselves. Perhaps over time they were free to look at the pattern in their excuses and eventually to take more responsibility. Furthermore, at the bottom of the Excuse Sheet below were clear but remedial consequences, which required them to fix the problem.

HOMEWORK EXCUSE SHEET

FOR ELEMENTARY STUDENTS

Name_____

Assignment:_____

Date_____

Due date was:_____

Here's why I didn't do my homework::

Teacher/Student Contract
a. 1/2 grade lower if turned in by the end of the school day
b. 1 grade lower if turned in tomorrow
c. 0 if **not** turned in
d. call to parents if 2 assignments with 0's

We have also provided a higher level excuse sheet, and further adaptations to each of these sheets could be made for younger elementary students and for older high school students.

HOMEWORK EXCUSE SHEET FOR

MIDDLE SCHOOL STUDENTS

Name_____

Assignment:_____

Date_____

Due date was:_____

This is why I didn't do my homework:

Teacher/Student Contract
a.   one grade lower if turned in by the
     end of the school day
b.   two grades lower if turned in tomor-
     row
c.   0 if not turned in
d.   call to parents if three assignments
     with 0's

Communicate with parents. Especially when new learning is required, parents want more information about your expectations, the purpose of your assignments, and an extensive two-way communication system, which would allow them to become partners in their child's instruction.[45] You have much to gain from parental involvement, which has been shown to:

1.   increase homework completion;

2.   increase attendance rates of students who avoid school;

3.   decrease disruptive behavior of students;

4.   improve students' attitudes toward school; and

5.   increase children's math and reading achievement .[46]

Teachers can inservice parents at the beginning of the year, at after-school meetings, or by newletters or booklets. Teachers report that such meetings were needed to give parents a sense of the context of instruction.[47] Almost half of the teachers in one study also asked parents for feedback about parent preferences and understandings of homework, using some of the following questions.[48]

Some Teachers Ask Parents About Homework

1.   Are you satisfied with the type and amount of homework your child is receiving?
2.   Do you feel homework is aiding your child's academic performance?
3.   What problems do your family and/ or your child encounter when doing homework?
4.   Are you able to help your child with his/her homework?
5.   What suggestions can you offer to improve our class's homework policies?

When parents were surveyed about the amount of homework their children received, half of them said their children got too much while the other half said they got too little. Parents who thought their children got too much homework felt that their children needed time for play and for their family.[49] Thus, your objectives and those of many parents can be met, if you make more assignments those that involve family members (e.g., cooking with fractions).

Communication is even more important when you have children with special needs included in your classroom. Parents of children with disabilities reported feeling unprepared to assist their children due to lack of information.[50] This was clearly stated by a parent:

"It would be helpful to have some parent sessions to inform us of techniques and purposes of homework, especially with the LD child. Sometimes I don't understand what my child is supposed to do and workbook sheets can be vague. It seems like the only time I hear from his teacher is when there is a behavior problem" (p. 182).[51]

You might consider having children bring projects/collections, observations, or stories that were generated at home into school--to use as (a) assessments of students, application of knowledge, (b) indicators of motivation, or (c) a way to integrate the curriculum with the daily lives of the students. Perhaps this is truly homework.

Summary. Your answers to the following questionnaire will help you pinpoint areas that can be used to improve your students' homework completion rates and attitudes. These answers are important for all your students. When applying your answers to students with special needs, it is reassuring to know that the majority of general educators believed that it was their responsibility to make adaptations of assignments for these students.[52] With the information we have provided related to general strategies, this should become an easier task.

POSITIVE TEACHER HOMEWORK PRACTICES

Assigning Homework

____ Yes ____ No   1. Do you use an outline of assignments and dates?

____ Yes ____ No   2. Do you make sure students have assignment books, homework planners, or homework buddies?

____ Yes ____ No   3. Do you make daily assignments at the beginning of the class rather than at the end?

____ Yes ____ No   4. Do you make sure the directions given to students about homework are clear by asking a student to repeat them or checking what is written down in assignment books?

____ Yes ____ No   5. Do you present instructions visually (overheads, on the board) as well as orally?

____ Yes ____ No   6. Do you provide assistance to students who have trouble organizing their materials at the end of the period or end of the day?

____ Yes ____ No   7. Do you provide assistance to students who have trouble sustaining attention by modifying the amount of work required of them?

Meaningfulness, Difficulty, and Length of Homework

____ Yes ____ No   1. Does the homework assignment overlap with lessons from the day?

____ Yes ____ No   2. Do you make homework assignments interesting to the students?

____ Yes ____ No   3. Do you talk about the purposes of an assignment?

____ Yes ____ No   4. Do you communicate to parents what is being taught and explain how parents can help?

____ Yes ____ No   5. Do you avoid assignments that require self-teaching or new learning?

____ Yes ____ No   6. Do you involve parents, other family members, or community resources in homework projects?

____ Yes ____ No   7. Do you use in-class study periods for elementary students?

____ Yes ____ No   8. Do you allow students with handwriting difficulties to use adaptations such as computers, notetakers, taped reports, printing, or reduced writing and copying?

____ Yes ____ No   9. Do you give asignments that are active as opposed to passive (e.g., gathering resources, interviewing persons, games, treasure hunts, observing natural phenomena)?

Collecting and Returning Homework with Feedback

____ Yes ____ No   1. Do you teach children who have difficulty returning homework how to graph percent of homework completed per day using colorful bars?

____ Yes ____ No   2. Are the rewards for completing homework as great as the consequences for not completing it?

____ Yes ____ No   3. Do you consistently grade homework or provide feedback to the student?

____ Yes ____ No   4. Do you give students incentives for completing homework, such as extra recess or class outings?

____ Yes ____ No   5. Do you have students turn in a written excuse for a missed assignment?

____ Yes ____ No   6. Do you allow a certain number of excused homework assignments (especially for students with special learning needs or with many after-school responsibilities)?

References

1. Polloway, E. A., Epstein, M. H., & Foley, R. (1992). A comparison of the homework problems of students with learning disabilities and non-handicapped students. <u>Learning Disabilities: Research and Practice, 7</u>, 203-209.
2. Cooper, H., & Nye, B. (1994). Homework for students with learning disabilities: The implications of research for policy and practice. <u>Journal of Learning Disabilities, 27</u>, 470-479.
3. Miller, D. L., & Kelley, M. L. (1991). Interventions for improving homework performance: A critical review. <u>School Psychology Quarterly, 6</u>, 174-185.
4. Cooper, H., & Nye, B. (1994). Homework for students with learning disabilities: The implications of research for policy and practice. <u>Journal of Learning Disabilities, 27</u>, 470-479.
5. Jenson, W. R., Sheridan, S. M., Olympia, D., & Andrews, D. (1994). Homework and students with learning disabilities and behavior disorders: A practical, parent-based approach. <u>Journal of Learning Disabilities, 27</u>, 538-548.
6. Murphy, J., & Decker, K. (1990). Homework use at the high school level: Implications for principals. <u>NASSP Bulletin, 74</u>, 0-43.
7. Roderique, T.W., Polloway, E.A., Cumblad, C., Epstein, M.H., & Bursuck, W.D. (1994). Homework: A survey of politics in the United States. <u>Journal of Learning Disabilities, 27</u>, 481-487.
8. Roderique, T.W., Polloway, E.A., Cumblad, C., Epstein, M.H., & Bursuck, W.D. (1994). Homework: A survey of politics in the United States. <u>Journal of Learning Disabilities</u>, 27, 481-487.
9. Murphy, J., & Decker, K. (1990). Homework use at the high school level: Implications for principals. <u>NASSP Bulletin, 74</u>, 40-43.
10. Murphy, J., & Decker, K. (1989). Teachers' use of homework in high schools. <u>Journal of Educational Research, 82</u>, 261-269.
11. Salend, S. J., and Schliff, J. (1988). The many dimensions of homework. <u>Academic Therapy, 23</u>, 397-403.
12. Polloway, E. A., Epstein, M. H., Bursuck, W. D., Madhavi, J., & Cumblad, C. (1994). Homework practices of general education teachers. <u>Journal of Learning Disabilities, 27</u>, 500-509.
13. Murphy, J., & Decker, K. (1990). Homework use at the high school level: Implications for principals. <u>NASSP Bulletin, 74</u>, 40-43.
14. Larson, R. W., & Richards, M. H. (1991). Boredom in the middle school years: Blaming schools versus blaming students. <u>American Journal of Education, 99</u>. 418-443
15. Bryan, T., & Nelson, C. (1994). Doing homework: Perspectives of elementary and junior high school students. <u>Journal of Learning Disabilities, 27</u>, 488-499. See also: Larson, R. W., & Richards, M. H. (1991). Boredom in the middle school years: Blaming schools versus blaming students. <u>American Journal of Education, 99</u>. 418-443
16. Murphy, J., & Decker, K. (1990). Homework use at the high school level: Implications for principals. <u>NASSP Bulletin, 74</u>, 40-43.
17. Cooper, H., & Nye, B. (1994). Homework for students with learning disabilities: The implications of research for policy and practice. <u>Journal of Learning Disabilities, 27</u>, 470-479.
18. Milkent, M. M., & Roth, W.M. (1989). Enhancing student achievement through computer generated homework. <u>Journal of Research in Science Teaching, 26</u>, 567-573.
19. Baumgartner, D., Bryan, T., Donahue, M., & Nelson, C. (1993). Thanks for asking: Parent comments about homework, tests, and grades. <u>Exceptionality, 4</u>, 177-185.
20. Nicholls, J. G., McKenzie, M., & Shufro, J. (1994). Schoolwork, homework, life's work: The experience of students with and without learning disabilities. <u>Journal of Learning Disabilities, 27</u>, 562-569.
21. Larson, R. W., & Richards, M. H. (1991). Boredom in the middle school years: Blaming schools versus blaming students. <u>American Journal of Education, 99</u>, 418-443.

22. Rosenberg, M. S. (1989). The effects of daily homework assignments on the acquisition of basic skills by students with learning disabilities. Journal of Learning Disabilities, 22, 314-323.
23. Bryan, T., & Sulivan-Burstein, K. (1997). Homework. Teaching Exceptional Children, July/August, 32-37.
24. Bryan, T., & Sulivan-Burstein, K. (1997). Homework. Teaching Exceptional Children, July/August, 32-37.
25. Rosenberg, M. S. (1989). The effects of daily homework assignments on the acquisition of basic skills by students with learning disabilities. Journal of Learning Disabilities, 22, 314-323.
26. VanSciver, J. H. (1990). Is more homework better? NASPP Bulletin, 74, 103-104.
27. Rosenberg, M. S. (1989). The effects of daily homework assignments on the acquisition of basic skills by students with learning disabilities. Journal of Learning Disabilities, 22, 314-323.
28. Bryan, T., & Sulivan-Burstein, K. (1997). Homework. Teaching Exceptional Children, July/August, 32-37.
29. Cooper, H. (1989). Synthesis of research on homework. Educational Leadership, 47, 85-91.
30. Murphy, J., & Decker, K. (1989). Teachers' use of homework in high schools. Journal of Educational Research, 82, 261-269. See also: Polloway, E. A., Epstein, M. H., Bursuck, W. D., Madhavi, J., & Cumblad, C. (1994). Homework practices of general education teachers. Journal of Learning Disabilities, 27, 500-509.
31. Polloway, E. A., Epstein, M. H., Bursuck, W. D., Madhavi, J., & Cumblad, C. (1994). Homework practices of general education teachers. Journal of Learning Disabilities, 27, 500-509.
32. Rojewski, J. W., Pollard, R. R., & Meers, G. D. (1992). Grading secondary vocational students with disabilities: A national perspective. Exceptional Children, 59, 68-76.
33. Polloway, E. A., Epstein, M. H., Bursuck, W. D., Madhavi, J., & Cumblad, C. (1994). Homework practices of general education teachers. Journal of Learning Disabilities, 27, 500-509.
34. Rojewski, J. W., Pollard, R. R., & Meers, G. D. (1992). Grading secondary vocational students with disabilities: A national perspective. Exceptional Children, 59, 68-76.
35. Beyda, S.D. & Zentall, S.S. (1998). Administrative responses to AD/HD. Reaching Today's Youth, 2, 31-36.
36. Polloway, E. A., Epstein, M. H., Bursuck, W. D., Madhavi, J., & Cumblad, C. (1994). Homework practices of general education teachers. Journal of Learning Disabilities, 27, 500-509.
37. Zentall, S.S., Harper, G., & Stormont-Spurgin, M. (1993). Children with hyperactivity and their organizational abilities. Journal of Educational Research, 60, 143-153.
38. Cooper, H., & Nye, B. (1994). Homework for students with learning disabilities: The implications of research for policy and practice. Journal of Learning Disabilities, 27, 470-479.
39. McLaughlin, T. F., Swain, J. C., Brown, M., & Fielding, L. (1986). The effects of academic consequences on the inappropri ate social behavior of special education middle school students. Techniques: A Journal for Remedial Education and Counseling, 2, 310-316.
40. Miller, D. L., & Kelley, M. L. (1991). Interventions for improving homework performance: A critical review. School Psychology Quarterly, 6, 174-185.
41. Rosenberg, M. S. (1989). The effects of daily homework assignments on the acquisition of basic skills by students with learning disabilities. Journal of Learning Disabilities, 22, 314-323.
42. Salend, S. J., and Schliff, J. (1988). The many dimensions of homework. Academic Therapy, 23, 397-403.
43. Polloway, E. A., Epstein, M. H., Bursuck, W. D., Madhavi, J., & Cumblad, C. (1994). Homework practices of general education teachers. Journal of Learning Disabilities, 27, 500-509.
44. Davis, S. J. (1990). 'The dog ate my homework' A middle school dilemma--and a solution. Middle School Journal, 21, 43.
45. Kay, P. J., Fitzgerald, M., Paradee, C., & Mellencamp, A. (1994). Making homework work at home: The parents perspective. Journal of Learning Disabilities, 27, 550-561.
46. Bryan, T., & Nelson, C. (1994). Doing homework: Perspectives of elementary and junior high school students. Journal of Learning Disabilities, 27, 488-499. See also: Cooper, H., & Nye, B. (1994).

Homework for students with learning disabilities: The implications of research for policy and practice. Journal of Learning Disabilities, 27, 470-479.

47. Kay, P. J., Fitzgerald, M., Paradee, C., & Mellencamp, A. (1994). Making homework work at home: The parents perspective. Journal of Learning Disabilities, 27, 550-561.

48. Salend, S. J., and Schliff, J. (1989). An examination of the homework practices of teachers of students with learning disabilities. Journal of Learning disabilities, 22, 621-623.

49. Baumgartner, D., Bryan, T., Donahue, M., & Nelson, C. (1993). Thanks for asking: Parent comments about homework, tests, and grades. Exceptionality, 4, 177-185.

50. Kay, P. J., Fitzgerald, M., Paradee, C., & Mellencamp, A. (1994). Making homework work at home: The parents perspective. Journal of Learning Disabilities, 27, 550-561.

51. Baumgartner, D., Bryan, T., Donahue, M., & Nelson, C. (1993). Thanks for asking: Parent comments about homework, tests, and grades. Exceptionality, 4, 177-185.

52. Polloway, E. A., Epstein, M. H., Bursuck, W. D., Madhavi, J., & Cumblad, C. (1994). Homework practices of general education teachers. Journal of Learning Disabilities, 27, 500-509. See also: Murphy, J., & Decker, K. (1989). Teachers' use of homework in high schools. Journal of Educational Research, 82, 261-269.